W9-CAE-962

Alexander Hamilton

Framer of the Constitution

Leaders of the American Revolution

Thomas Paine and the Fight for Liberty

John Adams American Patriot

Paul Revere Messenger for Freedom

Betsy Ross A Flag for a New Nation

Benedict Arnold Hero and Traitor

Alexander Hamilton Framer of the Constitution

Molly Pitcher Heroine of the War for Independence

Nathan Hale Courageous Spy

John Paul Jones American Naval Hero

George Washington America's Leader in War and Peace

Leaders of the American Revolution

Alexander Hamilton

Framer of the Constitution

Tim McNeese

CHELSEA HOUSE
PUBLISHERS
A Haights Cross Communications Company ®
Philadelphia

CHELSEA HOUSE PUBLISHERS
VP, NEW PRODUCT DEVELOPMENT Sally Cheney
DIRECTOR OF PRODUCTION Kim Shinners
CREATIVE MANAGER Takeshi Takahashi
MANUFACTURING MANAGER Diann Grasse

Staff for Alexander Hamilton
EXECUTIVE EDITOR Lee Marcott
EDITORIAL ASSISTANT Carla Greenberg
PRODUCTION EDITOR Noelle Nardone
PHOTO EDITOR Sarah Bloom
COVER AND INTERIOR DESIGNER Keith Trego
LAYOUT 21st Century Publishing and Communications, Inc.

A Haights Cross Communications ✦ Company ®

www.chelseahouse.com

First Printing

9 8 7 6 5 4 3 2 1

Library of Congress Cataloging-in-Publication Data

McNeese, Tim.
    Alexander Hamilton: framer of the Constitution/Tim McNeese.
      p. cm.—(Leaders of the American Reveolution)
    Includes bibliographical references and index.
    ISBN 0-7910-8616-X (hard cover)
  1. Hamiltion, Alexander, 1757–1804—Juvenile literature. 2. Statesmen—United
States—Biography—Juvenile literature. 3. United States—History—Revolution,
1775–1783—Juvenile literature. 4. United States—Politics and government—
1783–1809—Juvenile literature. I. Title. II. Series.
    E302.6.H2M44 2006
    973.4'092—DC22

                                                    2005004795

Contents

1 Caribbean Beginnings   1

2 A Brilliant Young Man   13

3 Patriot Origins   24

4 The Approach of Revolution   37

5 Through the Ranks   54

6 Love and Separation   69

7 Love and War   79

8 Constitutional Reformer   92

9 Directing the Nation's Economy   106

10 "Mine Is an Odd Destiny"   122

Chronology and Timeline   138

Notes   142

Bibliography   144

Further Reading   145

Index   147

Caribbean Beginnings

T oday, visitors to Washington, D.C., tour many of the important sites of the city, including the Washington Monument and the Jefferson Memorial, built and dedicated to honor the legacy and memory of two of America's Founding Fathers. These monuments command the landscape along the Tidal Basin and tower over the capital.

But a smaller legacy to another Founding Father often goes unnoticed. In the rotunda of the Capitol stands a seven-foot statue of one of the men who helped establish the United States: Alexander Hamilton.

He is, perhaps, the least understood of all of America's Founding Fathers. George Washington is remembered as the "Father of Our Country," for his leadership during the American Revolutionary War, and as the first president of the United States. Thomas Jefferson was the writer of the Declaration of Independence and America's third president, the one who purchased the vast territory of Louisiana from the French.

Alexander Hamilton never became president. He never even ran for the office. He came late to the revolutionary era, reaching the British colony of New York in 1772, just three years before the shooting began between the Americans and British at Lexington and Concord. He was younger than many of the remembered colonial leaders—Patrick Henry, Samuel Adams, John Dickinson. Such men had been in the colonies all or nearly all of their lives. When the British Parliament passed taxes on the colonies during the 1760s, it was men like Adams and Henry who protested.

Hamilton was a late arrival. He had been in America for only a short time before the Revolutionary War began. Yet, once the war started, Hamilton played an important role in helping to create the new national government and the nation called the United States. He served in the Continental Army, played a role in politics, helped create the United States Constitution, and served as America's first secretary of the treasury. His contributions were important, his words were defining, and his ideas were very timely. Yet Hamilton remains today an unknown figure, a seldom-remembered hero of the Revolution. Why?

Perhaps the answer lies in Hamilton's vision of America's future. Long before anyone else could see what the United States and its people would one day become, Hamilton saw it. Jefferson's vision of America's future was one in which power rested in the hands of landowning farmers, strong people who thought for themselves, and who wanted their government kept small and weak.

Hamilton, instead, was the champion of strong government, who did not trust the average, common man to make good political decisions. Hamilton wanted a strong national government presiding over a country

Alexander Hamilton believed that America's future success depended upon a strong national government and productive, industrial cities.

dotted by powerful productive cities with factories and manufacturing. Hamilton saw America's future in an expanding economy with powerful people making the important economic and political decisions.

During the late 1700s, Hamilton's vision was not popular with many Americans. Jefferson's, on the other hand, captivated the imaginations of thousands of American citizens. Jefferson's dream of early America was romantic. Hamilton's was about dollars and cents.

In the end, both visions of the future of the United States played their part in making America the nation it is today. But it is Hamilton's vision that seems most valid today, in a country dominated by large cities, a strong national government, and a tremendous amount of economic power held by large businesses and corporations.

Despite his visionary plans for America, Americans do not celebrate Hamilton. George Washington's birthday is a national holiday. Jefferson's home draws thousands of tourists each year, and his writings are frequently quoted. Yet America is, today, a place of Hamilton's making. It is Hamilton—honored simply with his face on the ten-dollar bill—who played an important role in not only creating the United States of his own time, but in helping to create the country the United States would one day become.

AN ISLAND HOME

Although Alexander Hamilton was a great American, he was born hundreds of miles from the colonies that he would one day help transform into the United States. Hamilton's first home was in the Caribbean Sea, on the tiny island of Nevis in the British Virgin Islands. The exact date of his birth is not known, but is believed to have been in January 1755. (Even the year of his birth is a subject of historical debate.)

There was no official record of Hamilton's birth. Hamilton's parents were not married to one another. His father was James Hamilton, a Scottish merchant in the islands. His mother, Rachel Fawcett Lavien, was married to another man, but had left him for James several years before Hamilton's birth.

Alexander Hamilton's father, James, was born in Scotland around 1718, the fourth of eleven children. His family lived in the ivy-covered Kerelaw Castle, which had become the family home in 1685. Although the castle is in ruins today, it included "a great hall with graceful Gothic windows."[1] Although James's brothers became successful—including two doctors, an apothecary, and a tobacco merchant—James became "the black sheep of the family, marked for mediocrity."[2] In 1737, at age 19, he was sent to a businessman in Glasgow to learn the merchant trade. Four years later, James Hamilton, his training completed, decided to migrate to the Americas and try his hand at trading in the West Indian islands. It was in the islands that he met Rachel. Two years before Alexander's birth, Rachel had given birth to another child, James, an older brother to young Alexander.

Nevis was "the merest speck of an island in the blue Caribbean,"[3] not a likely place for a great man to be raised. The Hamiltons lived in the island's capital, Charles Town. The island was small enough for Alexander and his brother to roam its beaches, dusty roads, and shanty houses, and know nearly everyone by name. From Charles Town, Alexander's father could carry on his business of buying and selling goods. Charles Town was a wealthy place. The sugar market produced lots of money. However, James Hamilton was never able to make a success of his business.

Little is known about Alexander Hamilton's early years. While he had some tutoring, he probably had little formal schooling. He learned French from his mother. One of his tutors may have been an elderly Jewish woman, according to a biography written by his son years later, after his father had become a famous man. During Hamilton's early years, one out of every four whites in Charles Town was Jewish. All through his life, Hamilton maintained a strong admiration for Jews, even though many people at the time did not.

The family of four remained together until 1765. That year, James Hamilton abandoned his common-law wife and their two sons. Rachel immediately set out to make a life for herself and her boys. By then, the family was living on another island, St. Croix, the largest of the Virgin Islands, in the town of Christiansted. (Today, St. Croix is U.S. territory.)

THE FAMILY BUSINESS

Alexander's mother soon went into buying and selling for herself and proved she "had a better head for business than her bankrupt 'husband.'"[4] With a small amount of money she inherited from her mother, Rachel set up a shop. She and her sons lived in a two-story house on 34 Company Street, near a church and a school. The small family lived upstairs and worked out of the store on the street-level first floor, selling food to planters—things like salted fish, beef, pork, apples, butter, rice, and flour.[5] Rachel kept a goat in her walled yard to provide milk for her family.

For three years, she ran a successful business. When Rachel opened up her store, Alexander was a bright ten-year-old boy. He seemed to have a good head for mathematics and figures, so his mother put him to work in her shop. Alexander was a clerk and helped keep records of the store's sales. It was here that young Alexander first entered the world of business and money. It would remain an area of interest his entire life.

While these were probably the best years of Alexander's youth, they did not last long. His mother died of yellow fever in 1768, just three years after his father had left the family.

For a while, a 22-year-old cousin, Peter Lytton, took in the two brothers. But new tragedy struck their lives when, in less than a year, Lytton committed suicide, having either stabbed or shot himself to death (history is not clear on the actual means of his death).[6]

Alexander and his brother, James, were 13 and 15 respectively, with no immediate family and no money.

Young Alexander learned difficult lessons during these years. He learned that he would have to work hard to make something of himself. He understood that nothing would ever come easy and life was uncertain. He would have to create his own place and his own name.

Alexander and James wasted little time. Their mother had shown them the value of hard work. Soon, James became the apprentice of a carpenter, so that he could learn a trade. In the meantime, Alexander, already experienced with business numbers and book records, hired on as a clerk to a New York merchant, Nicholas Cruger, who ran a trading business in St. Croix—the firm of Beekman and Cruger. (Hamilton's mother had stocked the shelves of her little Christiansted store with goods imported through Cruger's import and export business.) It would be young Alex's first connection to the place that would become his adult home—New York City.

Test Your Knowledge

I On what American currency does Alexander Hamilton's face appear?

   a. The one-hundred-dollar bill.

   b. The fifty-dollar bill.

   c. The ten-dollar bill.

   d. The quarter.

2 Where was Hamilton born?

   a. Virginia.

   b. Massachusetts.

   c. Scotland.

   d. Nevis.

3 How did Hamilton's father earn a living?

   a. He was a trader, buying and selling goods.

   b. He was a doctor.

   c. He was an apothecary.

   d. He was a farmer.

4 What job did Hamilton have in his mother's shop?

   a. He bought and sold goods.

   b. He was a clerk.

   c. He made the goods that his mother sold.

   d. None of the above.

5 After the deaths of his mother and cousin, who hired Hamilton?

a. A carpenter.

b. A shopkeeper.

c. A New York merchant.

d. A silversmith.

A Brilliant Young Man

Young Hamilton did well for his master and learned the finer points of bookkeeping and how to record business information. Hamilton's job as clerk in an important trading office in St. Croix placed him at the center of an active and busy coastal port. Ships sailed in and out of the harbor regularly, including not only merchant vessels but also an occasional pirate ship. Hamilton came in contact with sea captains and merchants from America and Europe. He met dockworkers from Africa, Central America, Brazil, and the Caribbean. He made deals with local plantation owners whose slaves grew sugar, molasses, and cotton.

Hamilton saw firsthand how inhumane slavery was. Even as a young man, he came to believe that slavery was wrong. Years later, as an adult, Alexander Hamilton helped establish an anti-slavery organization in New York.

In St. Croix, Nicholas Cruger provided Hamilton with experience in the business world. But he was not responsible for the care of the young man. That responsibility fell to a Scottish Presbyterian minister, the Reverend Hugh Knox. Soon after the death of Hamilton's mother, Knox became his teacher. Knox had immigrated to the Caribbean earlier from the American colonies. He had attended the College of New Jersey (today it is Princeton University), where he had studied religion under the college's president, Aaron Burr, Sr.

Reverend Knox taught his young charge not only spiritual matters, but other subjects as well. Hamilton's

Hamilton spent his early years living and working on the
island of St. Croix, the largest of the Virgin Islands, visible
in the background.

studies included literature and the sciences. (Reverend
Knox was also a part-time doctor.) The minister had a
large library, filled with books on everything from
history to Greek mythology. Hamilton was an interested

reader and, after coming home from Cruger's offices, often spent many hours reading. Hamilton also enjoyed writing, occasionally contributing letters and poetry to the local newspaper.

By the time he was 16, Hamilton was one of Cruger's most capable office employees. That year—1771—young Hamilton had an opportunity to prove just how valuable he was to his employer. By then, David Beekman had sold out of the trading firm. A prominent New Yorker, Cornelius Kortright, bought up Beekman's part of the business. That fall, Nicholas Cruger became very sick and left St. Croix, sailing to New York City.

Cruger's St. Croix trading office was part of a larger merchant business owned by Cruger's father and uncles. The Crugers owned trading offices through-out the Caribbean, as well as in Great Britain and New York. When Nicholas Cruger left, he turned the business over to Hamilton. For almost six months, the teenager ran the St. Croix office alone.

He handled things well and impressed the Cruger family with his abilities. But Nicholas Cruger returned to take up his responsibilities in St. Croix the follow-ing spring. Hamilton was soon back in his old job,

The Unknown Birthday

Alexander Hamilton has been the subject of research by historians for nearly two centuries. They have spent years collecting documents about Hamilton so that they can know more about this great man who became one of America's Founding Fathers. But while much is known about his adult years, little is known about the details of his early life. One of those simple details is when, exactly, was Alexander Hamilton born?

Until recent years, many historians placed the year of Hamilton's birth in 1757. But new evidence points historians to an earlier date. One significant piece of evidence is a court paper, dated 1768, stating that at the time, Hamilton was 13 years of age. Three years later, when he published a poem in a local St. Croix paper, Hamilton described himself as "a youth about seventeen,"[*] which was probably his way of saying he was sixteen and would turn seventeen on his next birthday. This means that he was born in 1755.

Although some later documents suggest that Hamilton was born in 1757, it appears likely that he was, in fact, born in 1755. At least one modern historian has determined not only the year, but also the month and day—January 11, 1755.

[*] Quoted in Ron Chernow, *Alexander Hamilton* (New York: Penguin Press, 2004), 17.

returning to "the grovelling and conditions of a Clerk."[7] At the age of 17, Hamilton was already beginning to look around, searching for a better place for himself. He was ready, as he wrote to a close childhood companion, Edward Stevens, to "prepare the way for futurity [the future]."[8] Hamilton did not realize it, but great change was in the wind for him.

THE GREAT ISLAND STORM

The opportunity for a different future for Alexander Hamilton came six months after Nicholas Cruger's return to St. Croix. On August 31, 1772, a violent hurricane hit the island, cutting a wide, destructive path. On an island where hurricanes were common, this storm was gigantic. A local newspaper reported the tropical storm as the "most dreadful hurricane known in the memory of man."[9] On Nevis, where Hamilton had been born, eyewitnesses reported that "huge sugar barrels were tossed four hundred yards, furniture landed two miles away."[10] In addition, a massive earthquake hit the islands on the same day, causing a 15-foot tidal wave to strike the beaches at St. Croix and the port of Christiansted. The storm destroyed so many of the islands that a relief effort was launched, and food was requested from the American colonies.

One week later, Hamilton wrote a long, emotional letter to his father. Even though James Hamilton had abandoned his son seven years earlier, father and son were still in touch. When shown the letter, Reverend Knox persuaded Hamilton to publish it in the *Royal Danish American Gazette*. Reluctantly, Hamilton agreed.

Readers were immediately impressed by the words written by the 17-year-old. The following is a portion of the published letter, dated October 3, about the storm:

It seemed as if a total dissolution of nature was taking place. The roaring of the sea and wind, fiery meteors flying about . . . in the air, the prodigious glare of almost perpetual lightning, the crash of the falling houses, and the ear-piercing shrieks of the distressed, were sufficient to strike astonishment into angels. A great part of the buildings through-out the Island are levelled to the ground, almost all the rest very much shattered; several persons killed and numbers utterly ruined; whole families running about the streets, unknowing where to find a place of shelter. . . . In a word, misery, in all its most hideous shapes, spread over the whole face of the country.[11]

As the letter continued, Hamilton saw the hand of God in the storm—"He who gave the winds to blow and the lightnings to rage."[12] But he ended the letter on a positive note. He gave God credit for rescuing him, and called on those with money to help those who had suffered terrible losses.

The letter caused an immediate response. Even the island's governor wanted to know the name of the young author of such a well-written, heartfelt letter. Such a brilliant youth needed to receive the best education possible, one unavailable in the islands. A fund was created to help provide money to send the talented Alexander Hamilton to college. Those who had already had an impact on Hamilton's youth contributed, including Nicholas Cruger, Cornelius Kortright, David Beekman, and Reverend Knox. These leading citizens of St. Croix began charting a new future for Hamilton. Perhaps, they thought, he might become a medical doctor and, one day, return to the islands. By early

1773, Alexander Hamilton, a 17-year-old orphan who had managed to impress nearly every adult who gave him a second glance, was on his way to America. He would never return to the West Indies.

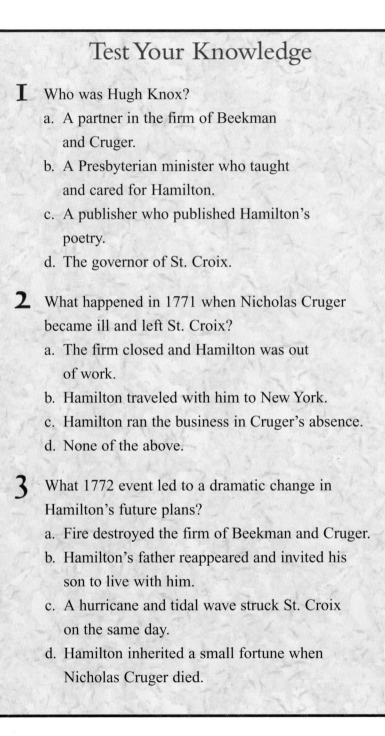

Test Your Knowledge

1 Who was Hugh Knox?

   a. A partner in the firm of Beekman
      and Cruger.

   b. A Presbyterian minister who taught
      and cared for Hamilton.

   c. A publisher who published Hamilton's
      poetry.

   d. The governor of St. Croix.

2 What happened in 1771 when Nicholas Cruger
became ill and left St. Croix?

   a. The firm closed and Hamilton was out
      of work.

   b. Hamilton traveled with him to New York.

   c. Hamilton ran the business in Cruger's absence.

   d. None of the above.

3 What 1772 event led to a dramatic change in
Hamilton's future plans?

   a. Fire destroyed the firm of Beekman and Cruger.

   b. Hamilton's father reappeared and invited his
      son to live with him.

   c. A hurricane and tidal wave struck St. Croix
      on the same day.

   d. Hamilton inherited a small fortune when
      Nicholas Cruger died.

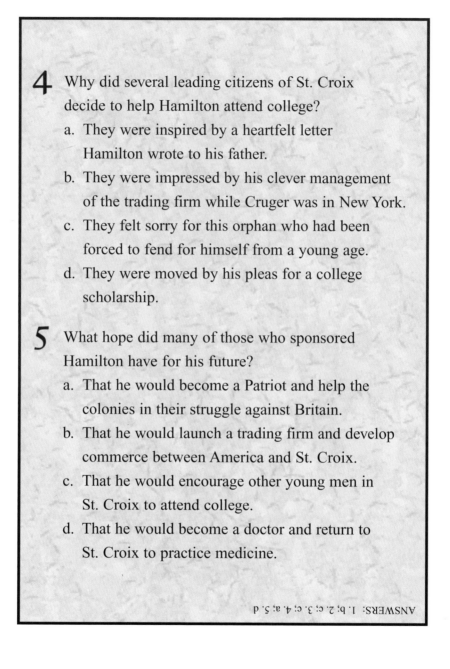

4 Why did several leading citizens of St. Croix decide to help Hamilton attend college?

   a. They were inspired by a heartfelt letter Hamilton wrote to his father.

   b. They were impressed by his clever management of the trading firm while Cruger was in New York.

   c. They felt sorry for this orphan who had been forced to fend for himself from a young age.

   d. They were moved by his pleas for a college scholarship.

5 What hope did many of those who sponsored Hamilton have for his future?

   a. That he would become a Patriot and help the colonies in their struggle against Britain.

   b. That he would launch a trading firm and develop commerce between America and St. Croix.

   c. That he would encourage other young men in St. Croix to attend college.

   d. That he would become a doctor and return to St. Croix to practice medicine.

ANSWERS: 1. b; 2. c; 3. c; 4. a; 5. d

Patriot
Origins

Alexander Hamilton's voyage to America took three weeks. The sea trip onboard one of Nicholas Cruger's ships proved more exciting than he expected. A fire broke out, and the crew was barely able to put it out in time. But the voyage continued, and Hamilton eventually reached Boston. Although he considered himself a loyal British subject, Hamilton found himself in a city filled with hatred for the British. For nearly a decade, British subjects in the 13 colonies had been protesting new taxes and customs duties. They protested the presence of thousands of British troops in their cities, including Boston (there was one British Redcoat in the city for every five Bostonians).

When Hamilton arrived, he discovered that a rebellion was dividing the colonists from Britain. For the moment, however, revolutionary politics were of no interest to Alexander Hamilton.

Hamilton did not remain in Boston for long. He soon rode a stagecoach over heavily rutted roads to New York City. Once in the city, Hamilton contacted friends of Nicholas Cruger, who helped smooth the way for his admission to school. Hamilton was interested in attending Princeton College in New Jersey. The school had originally been known as the College of New Jersey. In the 1750s, the college's second president had helped lead the effort to have the college moved to a new site. That campus was located in Prince Town. In time, the college was renamed Princeton. The president responsible for the move and renaming was Reverend Aaron Burr, Sr. He had taught Hamilton's mentor,

Reverend Knox; his son would one day become Hamilton's most famous opponent.

Before he was allowed to enroll at Princeton, Hamilton needed additional schooling. His sponsors had recommended that he attend Elizabethtown Academy in Elizabethtown, New Jersey, which was housed in a large two-story building, close to a Presbyterian church. (Today, the city is known as Elizabeth and is located just across the Arthur Kill River, west of Staten Island.) The school had a good reputation in the colonies. Hamilton studied under the respected Francis Barber, even though Barber was only a few years older than Hamilton himself. His subjects included Latin and Greek and several mathematics courses, including geometry.

Hamilton also studied independently, teaching himself French. He was a serious student, a quick learner who always enjoyed the challenge of new studies and subjects. He often worked past midnight, curled up in his blanket, then awoke at dawn and paced the nearby [church] burial ground, mumbling to himself as he memorized his lessons.[13] Hamilton's custom of pacing back and forth, talking to himself, would become a lifelong habit.

During his year of study in Elizabethtown, Hamilton stayed in the homes of friends of Cruger, including a lawyer named Elias Boudinot. Boudinot was a wealthy and influential man in New Jersey and New York politics. It was Boudinot who had helped organize and found Elizabethtown Academy, and who helped provide funds for poor, talented students, such as Alexander Hamilton. He and Boudinot became life-long friends.

In Boudinot's home, young Hamilton came in contact with important people, including the governor of New Jersey, William Livingston. He was soon under the influence of the supporters of the growing Patriot movement, especially Boudinot, who would become a leading New Jersey figure in the approaching American Revolution. Livingston, too, was a fiery writer on behalf of the Patriot cause, and was known by the nickname "the Whipping Post." [14]

COLLEGE DAYS

After one year of study, Hamilton believed that he was ready for college. Princeton was still his goal. It was, after all, the college Reverend Knox, his island mentor, had attended. He applied and met with college officials.

Hamilton was overly confident in this meeting, demanding that he be allowed to advance rapidly through his subjects and not be limited to the normal promotions from year to year. His request was not acceptable to the college trustees. Hamilton was surprised when his application was turned down.

But he did not waste time fretting about the denial. He soon applied to another school, King's College in New York. (Today, it is known as Columbia University.) King's College was, then, a small institution, with only three instructors, including the college's president. It was not as important a college as the other, better-known colleges in the colonies—schools like Harvard, Yale, and the College of William and Mary. But, once accepted, Hamilton moved to New York City and continued to be a very serious student.

Some of the time, Hamilton lived in the Boudinot home. At other times, he stayed with the Livingstons. The wealthy and powerful Livingston lived on a 120-acre estate called Liberty Hall. Although he had plenty of money and influence, Livingston was "a born crusader," a man who was naturally rebellious.[15] He worked against such Parliamentary measures as the Stamp Act and other attempts by Britain to restrict the colonies and force them to pay higher customs duties and taxes. He had a great and direct influence on Hamilton's political ideas and ideals.

While Hamilton was constantly stimulated by Livingston's words, he was also interested in other members of his family, including his children. Livingston's daughters were said to be beautiful and high-spirited. One of the daughters, Sarah Livingston, was so attractive and elegant that, while attending the Paris Opera, she was mistaken for the French queen. She would later marry John Jay, who became the first Chief Justice of the U.S. Supreme Court. Hamilton himself probably fell in love with another Livingston daughter, Catharine, who was "pretty, coquettish, somewhat spoiled, and always ready for flirtatious banter."[16] It was through the Livingstons that Hamilton met one of their cousins, Elizabeth Schuyler. Although she was too young at the time to draw Hamilton's attention, years later the two would fall in love.

When Hamilton began studying at King's College in 1774, New York City was in the midst of revolutionary politics. The question on many lips was focused on the future relationship between the 13

While studying in New York, Hamilton was a frequent guest at the home of the wealthy Livingston family. There he met Elizabeth Schuyler, who would later become his wife.

American colonies and the British king, George III. Hamilton was certainly exposed to this debate. While in the homes of Boudinot and Livingston, he heard many arguments calling for dramatic, even revolutionary change. But young Hamilton, new to America, did not immediately understand why so many colonists were upset with British authority. He would soon change his views.

THE MAKING OF A REVOLUTIONARY

Many of the issues of the day—taxation, customs duties, the power of Parliament, restrictions in colonial rights, issues regarding representation—were not, at first, important to Hamilton. When colonists protested the British tax on tea to the colonies, Hamilton did not understand all the fuss. He saw the tax as nothing more than "the petty duty of three pence on a pound of East India tea." [17]

In Boston, on December 16, 1773, rebel colonists, dressed as Mohawk Indians, threw 342 wooden chests of British tea into Boston Harbor rather than pay a small tax on the imported drink. In fact, it was after the famous "Boston Tea Party" that Hamilton decided to pay a visit to Boston and try to understand exactly what

On December 16, 1773, colonists dressed as Native Americans threw 342 chests of tea into Boston Harbor to protest the tax on the beverage.

was going on and why Bostonian rebels were so opposed to royal authority. In Boston, he talked to rebel leaders, including some of the more outspoken figures, such as Samuel Adams.

When Hamilton returned to New York City, he was a changed young man. Hamilton wrote an essay, titled "Defence of the Destruction of the Tea," which was soon published in a local Patriot publication, *Holt's Journal*. Pleased with seeing his words in print in support of the

Patriot cause, Hamilton then wrote a series of articles for the journal, which were well received.

During the summer of 1774, Hamilton expressed his opinions during a public meeting. On July 6, a gathering of Patriots was held at a site close to King's College, then called "The Fields." (Today, it is the site of New York's City Hall Park.) The purpose of the meeting was to protest the closing of Boston Harbor by the British Parliament, which had been done in response to the Boston Tea Party. The rally was well attended, and members of the local Sons of Liberty were present. A Liberty Pole had been erected, a symbol of Patriot freedom from British control.

After the leader of the meeting spoke in favor of a boycott against British goods, the crowd was not ready to go home. They called for another speaker. Soon, some of Hamilton's friends asked him to speak. One of his fellow club members shouted out, "Give 'em a speech, Alexander. You're good at it."[18] When other voices joined, calling for Hamilton to speak, the 19-year-old took the platform.

Gazing out over the sea of faces, he felt a kind of stage fright. It was the largest audience he had ever addressed, and he hesitated a moment, before his confidence returned. His voice grew strong and vigorous as he painted a picture of the long-oppressive actions of the mother country.[19]

His words easily won the crowd, and a cheer went up. Some asked who this young man was. Others answered, "It is a collegian!"[20] Young Alexander Hamilton, still only a college student, had made a public impression. He was now an outspoken, well-known voice for the Patriot cause.

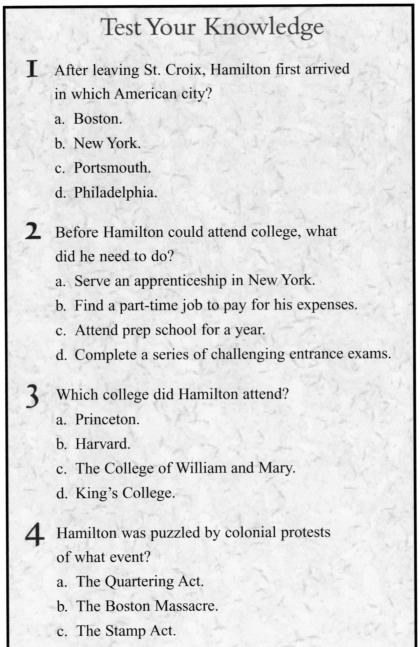

Test Your Knowledge

I After leaving St. Croix, Hamilton first arrived in which American city?

a. Boston.

b. New York.

c. Portsmouth.

d. Philadelphia.

2 Before Hamilton could attend college, what did he need to do?

a. Serve an apprenticeship in New York.

b. Find a part-time job to pay for his expenses.

c. Attend prep school for a year.

d. Complete a series of challenging entrance exams.

3 Which college did Hamilton attend?

a. Princeton.

b. Harvard.

c. The College of William and Mary.

d. King's College.

4 Hamilton was puzzled by colonial protests of what event?

a. The Quartering Act.

b. The Boston Massacre.

c. The Stamp Act.

d. The tax on tea.

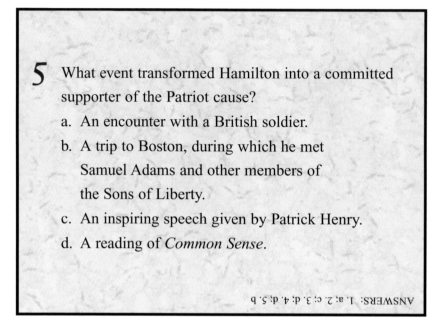

5 What event transformed Hamilton into a committed supporter of the Patriot cause?

a. An encounter with a British soldier.

b. A trip to Boston, during which he met Samuel Adams and other members of the Sons of Liberty.

c. An inspiring speech given by Patrick Henry.

d. A reading of *Common Sense*.

ANSWERS: 1. a; 2. c; 3. d; 4. d; 5. b

4

The Approach
of Revolution

Voices such as Hamilton's and others were gaining ground in New York and the outlying area. While there were Patriots in New York City, there were also many who wanted to remain loyal to Great Britain, favoring cooperation with the British government. These individuals were called Loyalists.

In November 1774, a Loyalist writer began publishing his views in local New York newspapers. His letters were written "anonymously" under the name "A Westchester Farmer." The writer actually was a local Anglican minister named Samuel Seabury. He was a highly educated man, who energetically supported Parliament in its policies toward the colonies. In these political letters, the Loyalist author was critical of the newly formed Continental Congress. This congress included members from many of the colonies, who were gathering in Philadelphia to discuss how to direct the growing conflict and division between the colonies and the British government. The letters were also critical of the ongoing boycott of British goods by Patriots. The boycott was designed to convince Parliament and the king to abandon their oppressive policies. In one letter, the anonymous critic described the leaders of the boycott as "a venomous brood of scorpions" who want to "sting us to death."[21] The writer stated that perhaps such individuals should "be greeted with hickory sticks."[22]

The local Patriots were immediately angered by the letters. Hamilton was furious, and wanted to express his response in print. The newspaper editor who had published the letters of "A Westchester Farmer" allowed Hamilton the opportunity to reply. By December, Hamilton published a pamphlet in the paper titled "A Full Vindication of the Measures of the Congress." Hamilton did not put his name on the letters (as was the custom of the day), but disguised himself as "A Friend to America." Hamilton's words demonstrated the heart of the Patriot cause, expressing that the struggle was against the tyranny of British authority:

> That Americans are intitled to freedom, is incontestible upon every rational principle. All men have one common original: they participate in one common nature, and consequently have one common right. No reason can be assigned why one man should exercise any power . . . over his fellow creatures more than another; unless they have voluntarily vested him with it. Since then, Americans have not by any act of their's impowered the British Parliament to make laws for them, it follows they can have no just authority to do it.[23]

With such words, Hamilton once again entered the public debate between Loyalists and Patriots. The debate between "A Westchester Farmer" and "A Friend to America" continued with other writings over the next few months. Within a few weeks of Hamilton's essay, Seabury responded with more letters, some of these attacking "A Friend of America."

Hamilton replied with an essay that was published in February 1775, titled "The Farmer Refuted." In this piece of writing, Hamilton continued to express his support for American freedom:

> I am inviolably attached to the essential rights of mankind, and the true interests of society. I consider civil liberty . . . as the greatest of terrestrial blessings. I am convinced, that the whole human race is intitled to it. . . . I verily believe also, that the best way to secure a permanent and happy union, between Great-Britain and the colonies, is to permit the latter to be as free, as they desire. To abridge their liberties, or to exercise any power over them . . . would be a perpetual source of discontent and animosity.[24]

These letters between a Loyalist and a fiery young Patriot represented an interesting war of words. They reveal how divided Americans were by the spring of

1775. When the year 1775 began, no one knew where this division would lead. Perhaps the Patriot cause might move past a refusal to obey English authority and break out into full-scale revolution. To do so would probably mean fighting and bloodshed. Hamilton hoped that such a development would not take place. In his first essay to Seabury, he wrote how it would be little more than "the grossest infatuation of madness" for Britain to "enforce her despotic claims by fire and sword."[25]

THE WAR BEGINS

Within two months of the publication of Hamilton's second essay responding to Seabury, American Patriots and British soldiers were at war with one another. On April 18, British Redcoats and Minutemen exchanged musket fire on the common at Lexington, Massachusetts, just outside of Boston. With these shots, the American Revolutionary War began. This war would bring dramatic change to the 13 colonies, as well as to the life of Alexander Hamilton.

Even before the April 1775 clash between Massachusetts Minutemen and British troops at Lexington and Concord, many of the students at King's

College, including Hamilton, had already joined volunteer fighting units, gathering in St. George's Chapel churchyard to drill before classes. They called themselves the Corsicans. Their "uniform" included a short, green coat and a small, rounded leather hat, cocked to one side, with the slogan, "Liberty or Death" stitched on it. Hamilton wore a small, heart-shaped pin that read: "God and our Right."[26] Hamilton drilled daily, and his classmates recognized him as an expert in the musket drill. The young students were caught up in "the military spirit."[27]

THE CORSICANS

Once the war began, Hamilton and his fellow Corsicans continued to drill as volunteer militiamen. The war spread outside Massachusetts, and militia units from all over the colonies sent men to Boston, where thousands of British soldiers were garrisoned. A Virginian named George Washington was chosen to command all the troops in the growing inter-colonial force, soon called the Continental Army. But Hamilton and his colleagues did not join them. They remained at King's College, having no orders from any higher authority.

By late June, Washington reached New York City, on his way to take command of the army gathered outside Boston. Already, a battle had taken place north of Boston, on Breed's and Bunker Hills, which had ended in a defeat for the colonial forces. Hamilton attended the public parade that marched down New York's Broadway, and got his first look at the Virginia general who would lead the American army through the Revolutionary War. In the military procession, another general, a wealthy New Yorker named Philip Schuyler, accompanied Washington. On that sunny, summer afternoon, Hamilton could not have known that, within two years, he would be serving as an aide to General

(continued on page 46)

In Support of Law and Order

Alexander Hamilton was caught up in the spirit of revolution in the spring of 1775. The thought of an armed rebellion excited him, and he quickly joined a volunteer militia unit. But he also understood that Patriot zeal could go too far. He did not support riots and the general destruction of private property. He did not support the actions taken by unruly mobs. On at least one occasion, he stood up against such a mob.

On April 25, one week after the fighting at Lexington and Concord, a group of fiery New York Patriots published a handbill threatening the life of the president of King's College, Dr. Myles Cooper. Cooper had remained loyal to Britain. Considered an important symbol of Tory power in New York City, Cooper had become a target for Patriot leaders, who wanted him to leave the city and his post at the college. Cooper refused.

Two weeks later, a mob of several hundred angry protesters, armed with clubs, marched through the streets to King's College with the intention of tarring and feathering him or riding him upon a rail.* A graduate of King's College spotted the angry mob and dashed ahead of them to warn Cooper to leave his campus lodgings through a back window. Alexander Hamilton and his roommate lived in a room close to Cooper's. They, too, were warned of the approach of the street mob. Hamilton made a quick decision, instantly resolving to wait on the outer stoop in front of Cooper's apartment and hold off the mob for as long as he was able, giving Cooper more time to escape.**

As the mob approached, Hamilton stood defiantly outside the president's lodgings. Before him stood more than 200 hotheaded Liberty Boys, who had already broken down the outer gate of the college yard. As they yelled loudly, Hamilton shouted them down. He told them that their conduct was wrong and that it would destroy their cause for liberty.

One version of the story includes a humorous sidenote. Still in his room, Cooper was uncertain what was going on outside his apartment. He raised his bedroom window while Hamilton was speaking. Partially deaf, he could not hear what was being said. Unaware that Hamilton was trying to help him, President Cooper is said to have shouted out: "Don't believe anything Hamilton says. He's a little fool!"*** Immediately, the mob broke into laughter.

Whether this particular scene took place remains in question. But one thing is clear: By standing in front of the mob, Hamilton was able to allow Cooper enough time to escape into the darkness, still dressed in his bedclothes. Hamilton, although a Patriot, could not give his support to a riotous mob that meant to do harm to a private citizen.

As for Cooper, he managed to escape to a British warship docked along the Hudson River. He soon left for England and never returned to America.

---

* Ron Chernow, *Alexander Hamilton* (New York: Penguin Press, 2004), 63.

** Ibid., 64.

*** Ibid.

(continued from page 43)

Washington, and that, one day, he would be married to the daughter of General Schuyler.

During the fall of 1775, Hamilton saw little activity as a volunteer. On August 23, he did participate in a bold mission. A British warship, *Asia*, was docked in the harbor. Nearby stood Fort George, manned by Patriot defenders. Afraid that the British might move on the fort and seize the two dozen cannon there, a group of over a dozen King's College students, including Hamilton, volunteered to remove the cannon. On the night of August 23, Hamilton and his classmates entered the fort and lashed the cannon with ropes, then began to drag the one-ton naval guns across the local common, in sight of the *Asia*. The small wheels on the guns squeaked, alerting the nearby British. When British troops on the ship spotted the students, they opened fire on them. Hamilton and his fellow students fired their muskets in return. Then, all 34 of the *Asia's* cannon cut loose a barrage of deadly grapeshot and cannonballs. A cannonball streaked through the night and hit the roof of Fraunces Tavern, a New York landmark that would become famous before the war's end. Even under fire, the King's College students managed to get ten cannon to safety that night.

Hamilton remained anxious to play an important role in the Revolutionary War. But his opportunity did not come immediately. Not until January 1776 did the New York Congress order the recruitment of an artillery company. Hamilton soon enlisted. With this enlistment, Hamilton left his college studies. He was appointed a captain of the artillery company.

A total of 68 men served under Hamilton's command. It was Hamilton's responsibility to keep the records of their enlistment and make certain that they were fed, clothed, and paid. He was also in charge of keeping discipline among them. When money failed to appear, he took some of his own private funds and used them to provide for his men. His men were put in charge of protecting colonial records stored in New York City. The assignment was boring and brought no action. But Hamilton's personal leadership of his men drew the attention of several senior officers. They noticed how Hamilton's men were well-trained and performed admirably during their parade exercises.

TOWARD INDEPENDENCE

By the summer of 1776, events began to turn quickly. In early July, the Continental Congress voted their

In early 1776, Hamilton became a captain in the New York artillery company. His skill and courage impressed General George Washington.

approval of the Declaration of Independence. This move changed the nature of the war with Great Britain. No longer were colonial troops fighting for their rights as Englishmen, but were fighting for their freedom from British rule. A week later, a British fleet of warships sailed up the Hudson, loaded with 34,000 British troops. That spring, Washington's army had routed the British out of Boston by placing cannon on the hillsides above the city. After the British evacuated the Massachusetts port city, Washington had moved his army to New York. The British, under the command of General William Howe, intended to force Washington out of the city.

Vastly outnumbered, Washington tried valiantly to hold onto New York City. But his inexperienced troops were no match for the well-trained and well-equipped British occupation force. (Washington's military leadership during this campaign was also no match for Howe's.)

At some time during the retreat of Washington's army from New York City, the commander-in-chief came in contact with Hamilton. During the retreat, Hamilton's artillery battery was part of the rear guard, helping to cover the advance of the Continental Army

Hamilton's artillery battery formed part of the rear guard during the Continental Army's retreat from New York.

out of the clutches of yet another British commander, Lord Charles Cornwallis. By moving into New Jersey, Washington's army was saved. As Washington wrote later, he was "charmed by the brilliant courage and admirable skill displayed by [Hamilton] who directed a battery against the enemy's advanced columns."[28]

The Continental Army was at a crossroads. Washington's forces were huddled against the winter snows in Pennsylvania. The year 1776 was rapidly approaching a close and the British army had won the upper hand at almost every turn. They had completed the capture of New York and were themselves in winter quarters in the city, living comfortably at the expense of the citizens of the city on the Hudson.

Test Your Knowledge

I   What pen name did Hamilton use for his published letters defending the Patriot cause?

     a. A Westchester Farmer.

     b. A Concerned College Student.

     c. A Friend to America.

     d. A Proud Patriot.

2   The King's College fighting unit was known by what name?

     a. The Corsicans.

     b. The Minutemen.

     c. The New York Militia.

     d. The Crusaders.

3   In August 1775, Hamilton and several other college students participated in a bold mission. What was it?

     a. To provide cover for Washington's troops as they marched out of New York.

     b. To launch an attack on the British warship *Asa*.

     c. To remove the cannon from Fort George.

     d. To capture British supplies from a storehouse near the Hudson River.

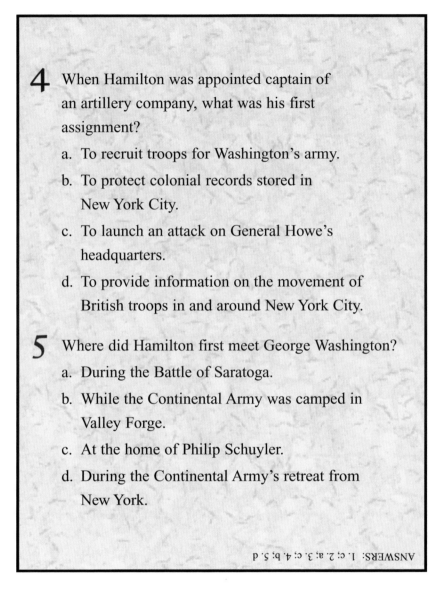

4 When Hamilton was appointed captain of an artillery company, what was his first assignment?

    a. To recruit troops for Washington's army.

    b. To protect colonial records stored in New York City.

    c. To launch an attack on General Howe's headquarters.

    d. To provide information on the movement of British troops in and around New York City.

5 Where did Hamilton first meet George Washington?

    a. During the Battle of Saratoga.

    b. While the Continental Army was camped in Valley Forge.

    c. At the home of Philip Schuyler.

    d. During the Continental Army's retreat from New York.

ANSWERS: 1. c; 2. a; 3. c; 4. b; 5. d

Through the Ranks

For Washington, it was a desperate time. Many of his men deserted, and more were preparing to leave his army, their terms of enlistment scheduled to end with the New Year. He felt he must make a decisive blow against the British before year's end and convince his men to remain with him. But how? Attacking New York was out of the question. The nearest garrison of enemy forces—mercenary troops from Germany called Hessians—was across the Delaware River in the small town of Trenton, New Jersey. Washington decided to launch an attack there. He set the date for December 25, knowing that the German soldiers would be celebrating Christmas by drinking heavily.

That December, Hamilton's artillery unit was encamped with the main body of Washington's forces. On the afternoon of Christmas, many of Washington's troops were roused from their quarters, including Hamilton and his cannoneers. He and his men were soon part of a long column of Continental soldiers moving single file toward a road leading to

(continued on page 58)

Hamilton and Burr's First Encounter

While Alexander Hamilton and Aaron Burr will always be remembered for their famous duel, the two men had known each other for 30 years before that encounter. During the American Revolution, they both served in the Continental Army. On at least one occasion, their paths may have crossed during the conflict.

As the British pressed Washington's army during the long battle for control of New York City in August 1776, Hamilton was serving under the command of one of Washington's generals, Israel Putnam. Washington had dispatched Putnam's men to Brooklyn Heights. There, Putnam and his officers soon realized that they would not be able to defend their position, given the strength of British opposition. But they remained, and British General William Howe attacked on August 27. Howe overwhelmed Putnam's forces, placing them in harm's way between his army and the British fleet. Washington ordered Putnam to move his men in retreat across the river to Manhattan Island.

The watery retreat was difficult. But Hamilton oversaw the ferrying of his cannon across the river. Once across, Hamilton placed his men in a small fort named Bunker's Hill. But he and his men had not reached complete safety. To remain in the fort would be suicide, as Howe's men were continuing to advance. Unwilling to retreat further and uncertain where to retreat to safely, Hamilton and his artillery unit remained in the fort. Capture seemed inevitable. Inside the fort, Hamilton was under the direct command of General Henry Knox, who had also reached its walls. (Knox and Hamilton would one day serve together in the presidential cabinet of George Washington.)

Confusion reigned inside the fort. Then, into the fort rode one of Putnam's other junior officers, Aaron Burr. Burr was a major, a young man only a year older than Hamilton. In the action, Burr had been cut off from his own men. Discovering that Knox did not know where to move next, Burr confidently announced that he knew the roads and could lead the men to safety.

Despite Burr's assurances, General Knox intended to stay where he was. Burr then turned away from General Knox and spoke directly to the men in the fort: "Do you wish to remain here and end up in a dungeon or hung like dogs or will you follow me who can bring you to safety? Better that half of you die bravely fighting than all of you be sacrificed like cowards."[*] Among those who heard these words was Alexander Hamilton. Soon, many of Knox's men were ready to follow Burr and leave their commander behind. Reluctantly, Knox agreed to Burr's offer. Hamilton did the same. Burr then led his fellow Patriot soldiers along an unused back road to safety into Washington's main lines.

[*] Quoted in Nathan Schachner, *Alexander Hamilton* (New York: Thomas Yoseloff, 1957), 51.

(continued from page 55)

a local river crossing—McKonkey's Ferry. The day was cold, and even when the column stopped marching, they were not allowed to light any fires. Campfires might alert the enemy of their presence. Hamilton and his men sat down to a cold meal. At their side stood a pair of their cannon. Once darkness fell, the Patriot forces were again on the march, each reaching the banks of the Delaware in their turn. Only then were they informed of their mission: To cross the river into British-held New Jersey and attack the sleeping Hessian garrison. The infantry was to cross first; artillery units, such as Hamilton's, were to cross last.

Around 11:00 P.M., the weather took a nasty turn, as the wind began to rise, and the snow began to fall heavily. This slowed down the movement of units sent toward the river. Hamilton and his men waited another hour before his company was called up to the riverbank. He ordered his cannon forward, the snow muffling the sound of the cannon's pair of wheels. As he and his men approached the ferry site, they loaded their guns on an oddly shaped barge, called a Durham boat, which measured 60 feet long and only six feet wide. With great difficulty, the guns were

Hamilton's artillery unit was with Washington as he crossed the Delaware River and attacked Hessian soldiers based in Trenton, New Jersey.

loaded onto the barge, pulled on deck by teams of horses. The deck was slippery, and the rocking boat made the horses nervous. As Hamilton looked out across the water, he "saw jagged chunks of ice that seemed to increase in size even while the swift current swept them momentarily into and out of his field of vision."[29]

At the ferry site, the river crossing was less than a quarter of a mile. But ice coated the boat deck, and the current fought against the barge, trying to force it downstream. Once the crossing was completed, Hamilton and his men unloaded their cannon with as much difficulty as they had loaded them on the opposite bank of the Delaware River. More time passed. Then, around 3:00 A.M., Hamilton received specific orders. He was to march his small artillery unit over the eight miles to Trenton and attack the unsuspecting Hessian garrison. Surprise was the watchword. There should be little noise, and no lights allowed. The weather howled around them, and snow and wind made it difficult for horses and soldiers to move forward. They slipped frequently on the snow and ice. They paused briefly at Birmingham to eat some cold food. The soldiers ate standing up; those who sat down were in danger of freezing to death.[30]

THE BATTLE BEGINS

At Birmingham, the advancing army split into two forces, one marching to the right following the road leading straight into Trenton. Hamilton's unit continued forward, swinging around to approach the Hessian garrison from a different direction. A few more hours passed. Then, just before 8:00 A.M., as the first rays of morning daylight were visible on the horizon, Hamilton heard distant musket fire. Hamilton and those around him began to advance faster, wanting to reach the action. The Continentals moved to the top of a hill, which looked down over the small townscape of Trenton. Here Hamilton could see the two main streets of the town that flanked the northern banks of the Delaware River. Lining the streets were a few dozen two-story houses, storefronts, and taverns. In the center of the town, between the two roads, stood St. Michael's Church, its white pillars facing toward the American artillery batteries to the north. As Hamilton's men moved forward toward the westernmost street, they saw American artillery units already in place, blasting down the easternmost main road. Behind them was Washington's main force, the commander-in-chief at their side.

Continental forces were approaching the sleepy town from every direction of the compass, surrounding the Hessians. Musket fire could be heard everywhere. Hamilton's men scrambled to move their two artillery pieces into place facing King Street. In the dim light of the early morning, Hamilton could see that the street was nearly empty, except for a few surprised Hessians who staggered groggily about, uncertain of what was taking place. Just as Hamilton's cannon were readied, a large Hessian detachment came into view, attempting to move into military formation, "their metal helmets and upraised bayonets gleam[ing] against the grayish-white of air and ground."[31] The same heavy snows that had nearly blinded the advancing Continentals through the night now did the same for the Hessians. The advancing Hessian column headed straight toward Hamilton's cannon, failing to see the artillery unit.

Hamilton gave the order to fire his two cannons. Bodies soon littered the snowy ground along King Street. Those Hessians who had not fallen took cover in an alley. Suddenly, eight Hessian horses appeared out of the snowy fog, pulling two enemy cannon. Before Hamilton could respond, the cannon returned fire, aiming directly at his artillery battery. At almost the same moment, Hamilton ordered his men to fire off a second round. Cannon shot flew past Hamilton and his men, but made no direct hits. However, opposing Hessians fell, as well as several of their horses. After firing off one more cannonade, this time of grapeshot, the Hessians manning the artillery battery opposite Hamilton's turned and fled toward the relative safety of the town. Other Americans rushed forward, manned the abandoned German cannon, and turned them around to face the fleeing Hessians.

Washington's plan to surprise his enemy and bring about a victory, despite a raging snowstorm and treacherous river crossing, was suddenly a reality. And Hamilton had played his role efficiently and effectively. The Christmas battle ended with lopsided results. The Continentals captured nearly 1,000 Hessians and an equal number of stands of arms. In addition, they seized six brass artillery pieces.

Hamilton admired the captured cannon. They were the best he had ever seen. On the American side, only two soldiers were killed and four wounded. As a result of the Trenton victory, other German garrisons scattered throughout the New Jersey countryside also surrendered.

ON TO PRINCETON

Washington wasted few days before he began to advance further into British-held territory. As for the

British, they were advancing, as well. General Lord Cornwallis, who had celebrated his thirty-eighth birthday less than a week after the battle of Trenton, advanced across New Jersey toward Washington's army. Soon, Cornwallis caught up with the Virginia general, pinning him down between Trenton and Assunpink Creek, a tributary of the Delaware. Having no boats available to evacuate across the river to safety, Washington found his forces in a tight spot. But on the night before Cornwallis intended to advance and do battle, Washington found a way around his enemy.

Through the night of January 2, Washington evacuated his men. To fool the British, he ordered campfires left burning and one artillery company to fire at any approaching British troops. Moving around Cornwallis's left flank, Washington and his army headed for a British garrison at nearby Princeton. Engaging two British regiments in a pitched battle in an open field, the Continentals sent them into full retreat. Washington surprised a third British regiment, which was hiding in a brick building on the campus of the College of New Jersey in Princeton. After an American cannonball was shot through a window, the Redcoats inside immediately surrendered. The cannonball struck a painting on the wall, decapitating the head of the portrait's subject— King George II. According to legend, the cannonball was fired by Alexander Hamilton.

Within days, Washington had managed to win two small, but highly symbolic battles on New Jersey soil. The victory encouraged the Patriot cause as a new year of the revolution—1777—began. Hamilton emerged from the wintry campaign as a seasoned artillery officer.

Hamilton and his men had performed well. His company remained disciplined because they knew that was what their commander expected. He served as their prime example. One eyewitness observed Hamilton during the fighting over New York City as "a youth, a mere stripling, small, slender," marching "beside a piece of artillery, with a cocked hat pulled down over his eyes, apparently lost in thought, with his hand resting on a cannon, and every now and then patting it, as if it were a favorite horse or a pet plaything."[32]

In the weeks that followed the raids on Trenton and Princeton, Washington asked Hamilton to become one of his personal aides. Washington explained that he needed "someone who can think for me as well as execute orders."[33] As an incentive, he offered Hamilton the rank of lieutenant colonel. Hamilton soon accepted Washington's offer, taking up his new commission on March 1, 1777. The Revolutionary War would continue for another four years, and the world was only beginning to take notice of Alexander Hamilton.

Test Your Knowledge

1 Why was the attack on the Hessian soldiers at Trenton so critical for Washington?

   a. Many of his men were scheduled to leave the army at the end of the year.

   b. A new commander-in-chief had been appointed to replace him.

   c. The Continental Congress was preparing to draft terms of surrender to the British.

   d. None of the above.

2 Why did Washington select December 25 as the date for the attack?

   a. He knew that the Hessians would be in church and unprepared for a battle.

   b. He wanted to attack earlier, but had to wait until the weather conditions became more favorable.

   c. He knew that the Hessians would have been drinking heavily on Christmas Eve.

   d. He knew that the British were preparing an attack on his troops on December 26, and so wanted to strike first.

3 What role did Hamilton's unit play in the battle at Trenton?

    a. They led the first attack, using bayonets to push back the Hessian forces.

    b. Mounted on horseback, they charged through the fleeing Hessians, forcing them toward the river.

    c. They fired rifles.

    d. They fired cannons.

4 One legend says that a cannonball fired by Hamilton at British soldiers struck a portrait on a wall, cutting off the subject's head. Who was the subject of the portrait?

    a. George Washington.

    b. King Henry VIII.

    c. King George III.

    d. King George II.

5 After the raids on Trenton and Princeton, what role did Washington offer Hamilton?

    a. He promoted Hamilton to general.

    b. He promoted Hamilton to lieutenant colonel and made him one of his personal aides.

    c. He offered Hamilton the position of Secretary of the Treasury in his first presidential cabinet.

    d. He asked Hamilton to serve as his press officer.

ANSWERS: 1. a; 2. c; 3. d; 4. d; 5. b

Love and Separation

It was the spring of 1777, and Lieutenant Colonel Alexander Hamilton had risen to great heights of influence and power. Only five years earlier, he had sailed to the British colonies from the island of St. Croix as a teenaged shipping clerk, uncertain of his future. Although he could not be certain that spring whether the American Revolution

69

would end favorably for him and the young United States, he could be proud of what he had accomplished. His actions as an artillery captain had gained him the attention of General Washington. Washington's advancement of young Alexander to aide-de-camp gained Hamilton the attention of influential people in New York. Without question, Hamilton's star was rising.

That spring, Washington's army saw little action. The commander-in-chief watched the enemy closely, trying to determine the next step taken by the British general William Howe. During that time, Hamilton had the opportunity to develop his professional relationship with Washington. He quickly became Washington's most capable aide, similar to a chief of staff. Hamilton stayed busy writing letters to Congress, to governors, and to Washington's generals. He even issued orders in Washington's name. One general described the importance of Hamilton's service to General Washington: "During the whole time that he was one of the General's aides-de-camp, Hamilton had to think as well as to write for him in all his most important correspondence."[34]

By late summer, Howe finally moved his 15,000 Redcoats toward Philadelphia, intending to capture the city, which was home to the Continental Congress. Washington moved against him, engaging Howe's army at Brandywine Creek, Pennsylvania, south of the city, on September 11, and again at Germantown on October 4. Outnumbered and, at Germantown, out-maneuvered, Washington lost both battles and watched helplessly as the British occupied Philadelphia, forcing the delegates to the Continental Congress to flee for their lives.

Despite these field losses, the Americans did achieve a victory in October. Another army, under the direct command of General Horatio Gates, defeated a major British force commanded by General Johnny Burgoyne in upstate New York. The Battle of Saratoga, occurring two weeks after Washington's loss at Germanton, was an important victory.

WINTER AT VALLEY FORGE

A few months later, as the temperatures began to drop, Washington's troops moved into their winter quarters at Valley Forge, Pennsylvania, where they would spend a miserable season. The troops were not pro-vided enough food or clothing for the winter. As one soldier described the army's condition by January:

"Twenty-six in one York regiment have been three weeks without a shirt. One fourth of our men now barefoot without blankets or breeches, lying uncovered in the field."[35]

Hamilton worked closely with Washington on the problems of food supply and clothing, appealing constantly to Congress for more support. But support remained scarce. The Congress simply did not have money enough to support its men in uniform.

By the spring of 1778, the remnants of the Continental Army emerged from their terrible winter experience ready to fight. In late June, General Clinton began to remove his British troops from Philadelphia. France had entered the conflict as an ally of the Americans. A French fleet was headed for Philadelphia. To avoid being trapped in the city, Howe decided to leave.

Following Howe, Washington ordered an attack at Monmouth Courthouse, New Jersey, on the rear of Howe's advancing line. Hamilton's role in the fight was limited. He was ordered ahead to scout out British field positions. The result of the fight was a small victory for Washington. During the fighting, an enemy musket ball wounded Hamilton's horse.

The Monmouth engagement would become the last significant battle for Washington's army until the end of the Revolutionary War. Much of the fighting taking place over the next three years was concentrated in the southern states. There, the British faced other American armies, while Washington remained in the north. These years proved frustrating for Hamilton. He was anxious for combat. But most of the action he saw took place at the beginning of the war and at its end.

A NEW LOVE

The years between 1778 and 1781 brought much change to the life of Alexander Hamilton. Since Washington's army fought little during this time, Hamilton had some time for other diversions. One was a young lady, Elizabeth Schuyler, the daughter of one of Washington's generals. In 1780, while the army was encamped at Morristown, New Jersey, 22-year-old Elizabeth visited the army, where she came into contact with 25-year-old Hamilton. The two had actually met three years earlier, in 1777, when Hamilton was sent by Washington to meet with General Gates after the battle of Saratoga. (Hamilton might have met Elizabeth before the war

Hamilton's Economic Ideas Begin

During the years of relative inactivity for Washington's army—from 1778 to 1781—Hamilton began to show an interest in the finances of his new country. As a young man, he had always had a head for numbers and figures. In 1779, he began promoting the idea of a national bank, partially funded by private citizens. The bank would provide an available money source for Congress. Such an important institution would tie "the interest of the State in an intimate connection with those of the rich individuals belonging to it."[*]

But a national bank never became reality during the war. The new national government existed under a new constitution—the Articles of Confederation. This document gave great power to the states and little to the national government.

Hamilton did not like having power held by the states at the expense of the national government. It was a position he would hold for the rest of his life. One day, he would help change that imbalance. But throughout the war, his economic ideas remained unaccepted and untested.

[*] Quoted in Nancy Whitelaw, *More Perfect Union: The Story of Alexander Hamilton* (Greensboro, N.C.: Morgan Reynolds Publishing, Inc., 2003), 38.

While Washington's army was encamped at Morristown, New Jersey, Hamilton fell in love with Elizabeth Schuyler. They married in December 1780; George Washington hosted a reception for the newlyweds.

while living with the Livingstons. She was a cousin to the Livingston daughters.)

Hamilton, it appears, was ready for marriage. When reintroduced to Elizabeth, he quickly fell in love. One of his fellow aides-de-camp soon noticed a change in him, saying, "Hamilton is a gone man."[36]

Elizabeth was everything that Hamilton wanted in a woman. She had qualities others easily noticed, including a visiting Frenchman, who noted that she was "a delightful woman who combines both the charms and attractions and the candor and simplicity typical of American womanhood."[37]

Hamilton was soon exchanging letters with Elizabeth. In one, he wrote: "For you must always remember your best friend is where I am."[38]

When Elizabeth, who was known to friends and family as Betsey, informed her parents of Hamilton's interest in her, they visited Washington's encampment in the spring of 1780. They found Hamilton acceptable as a match for their daughter, and wedding plans were set for later in the year.

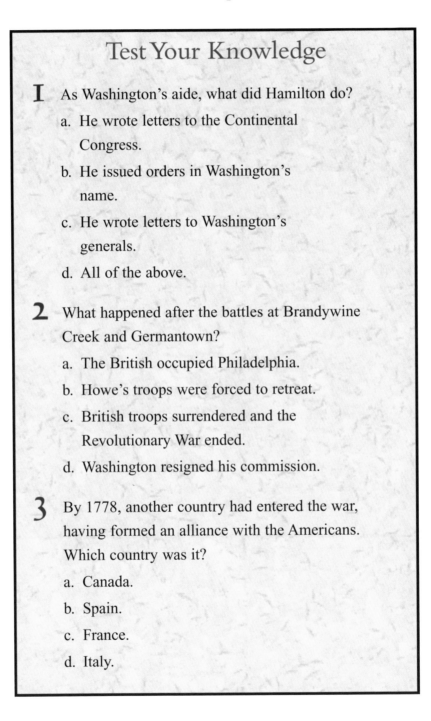

Test Your Knowledge

1 As Washington's aide, what did Hamilton do?

a. He wrote letters to the Continental Congress.

b. He issued orders in Washington's name.

c. He wrote letters to Washington's generals.

d. All of the above.

2 What happened after the battles at Brandywine Creek and Germantown?

a. The British occupied Philadelphia.

b. Howe's troops were forced to retreat.

c. British troops surrendered and the Revolutionary War ended.

d. Washington resigned his commission.

3 By 1778, another country had entered the war, having formed an alliance with the Americans. Which country was it?

a. Canada.

b. Spain.

c. France.

d. Italy.

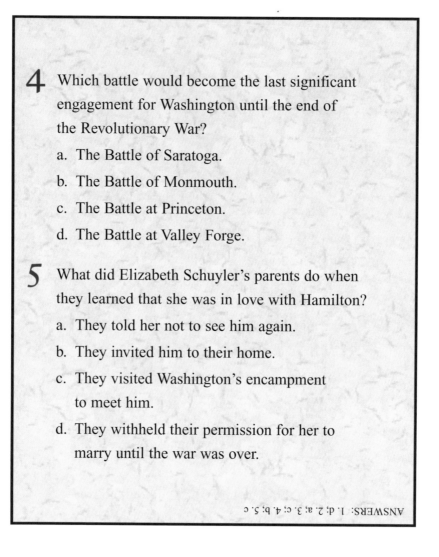

4 Which battle would become the last significant engagement for Washington until the end of the Revolutionary War?

a. The Battle of Saratoga.

b. The Battle of Monmouth.

c. The Battle at Princeton.

d. The Battle at Valley Forge.

5 What did Elizabeth Schuyler's parents do when they learned that she was in love with Hamilton?

a. They told her not to see him again.

b. They invited him to their home.

c. They visited Washington's encampment to meet him.

d. They withheld their permission for her to marry until the war was over.

ANSWERS: 1. d; 2. a; 3. c; 4. b; 5. c

Love
and War

Despite the plans for his marriage to Betsey, the year 1780 would prove difficult for Hamilton. There was inactivity within Washington's army while Hamilton longed for battle. The Congress did not give enough support to the Continental Army, which suffered constantly from a lack of food, clothing, supplies, equipment, ammunition, and pay.

These realities wore on Hamilton. The Articles of Confederation were failing the military and the people in general, Hamilton believed. They did not hold enough power to adequately lead the new nation.

Even before the Revolutionary War was over and the independence of the new United States assured, Hamilton began campaigning, in his writings and through various powerful men he knew, for a change in the national government.

The year was also marred by the discovery that one of Washington's generals, Benedict Arnold, had attempted to hand over plans for the military fortress at West Point, on the Hudson River, to the British in exchange for money. The discovery of this traitor both frustrated and angered General Washington, as well as Hamilton. The incident also caused a wedge between Washington and Hamilton. Arnold had an accomplice, a British soldier named Major John Andre. When Andre was captured (Arnold managed to escape and fled to England), he was tried and sentenced to death as a spy. Washington ordered him hanged. Hamilton believed a firing squad was a more humane and digni-fied way for an officer and gentleman, even an enemy, to be executed.

By December 1780, Hamilton and Elizabeth Schuyler were married. The ceremony took place in the Schuylers' Albany mansion. The bride and groom stood before a grand fireplace in the family's blue drawing room. Betsey wore a white wedding dress and Hamilton wore a black velvet coat with white satin knee breeches and a white, powdered wig, which was the fashion of the day. Since the wedding took place near Christmas, holly branches were used as decoration.

The marriage came at a time of redirection in Hamilton's life. He was becoming frustrated. The war was dragging on. The government seemed unable to solve even the simplest national problems. He wanted to be, as he had from the war's beginning, where the action was, longing for a field command. But Washington repeatedly refused him.

Hamilton was uncertain about his own future, as well. Would he play an important role in the new nation he was helping, in some small way, to establish? What would he do in the future to leave his mark on the world? He expressed his frustration in a letter to a colleague, writing, "I hate Congress—I hate the Army—I hate the world—and I hate myself. The whole is a mass of fools and knaves."[39]

(continued on page 84)

An Early Duel

While Hamilton is often remembered for engaging in a duel with Aaron Burr, that conflict was not his first dueling experience. During the Revolutionary War, Hamilton participated in a duel involving another of Washington's aides-de-camp.

In the eighteenth and early nineteenth centuries, dueling was common practice. If the words or actions of one man offended the personal honor of another, he might quickly be challenged to settle the matter with the weapon of his choice.

Hamilton was one of several young men who served as aides to General Washington. Another was John Laurens of South Carolina. Laurens had joined the Continental Army in 1777 and was wounded at the Monmouth engagement. A fearless soldier and officer, Laurens became Hamilton's close friend. Following the Monmouth battle, Laurens challenged one of Washington's generals to a duel. General Charles Lee had performed poorly, almost cowardly, at Monmouth. He had also been an outspoken critic of Washington. He often blamed Washington for his own failures on the field. Tiring of Lee, Laurens challenged him to a duel in December 1778.

Those who engaged in a duel selected a friend to assist them, a role called a "second." The seconds of two duelists usually became their spokesmen, sending messages back and forth, determining when the duel might take place. The duel was set for 3:30 P.M. on December 23. Laurens and Lee both selected dueling pistols as their weapon of choice, agreeing to advance and fire at will.

On the day of the duel, Hamilton accompanied Laurens to the site, on the edge of woods outside Philadelphia. As the duelists faced one another, they approached. When they stood about five or six paces apart, they both fired their pistols. Laurens shot Lee, who fell from his wound. Laurens, Hamilton, and Lee's second, Major Edwards, rushed toward Lee. The wounded general brushed off the wound, and wanted to exchange a second round of shots. Both Hamilton and Edwards insisted that the duel should be ended. Lee continued to protest.

As the four men discussed the argument that had led to the duel, Lee made it clear that he did not dislike Washington, and had not intended to criticize him personally. He had only criticized some of Washington's military decisions, which he said he had a right to do. Laurens found Lee's explanation acceptable, and the duel came to an end.

(continued from page 81)

Hamilton's growing dissatisfaction finally led him to quarrel with Washington. Within two months of his marriage, the general and his aide engaged in a serious argument, which left Hamilton offended and angry. Although Washington did apologize for expressing undue anger at his trusted and loyal aide, Hamilton decided that the time had come to leave Washington. In April, Hamilton left Washington's service. Almost immediately, he applied for a field command, sending the application directly to his old commander-in-chief. But Washington refused, explaining that the appointment would make him vulnerable to accusations of favoritism.

That spring, Hamilton learned that Betsey was pregnant. During the months that followed, Hamilton looked forward to the arrival of his child. He told Betsey that he really wanted a boy. He spent much of the summer of 1781 writing a series of anonymous essays, which he submitted under the title "The Continentalist." The papers were published in several New York newspapers. In these editorials, Hamilton continually called for a stronger national government. As a soldier and aide to Washington, he had seen what happened when the Congress operated without the power it needed. He listed the powers he believed a strong government should have over the states, most importantly, the power to tax its people and conduct trade.

A NEW COMMAND

By the end of the summer, General Washington finally agreed to give Hamilton command of a New York regiment. The timing was important. By the fall of 1781, the British had been virtually driven out of the American South, having suffered a serious of defeats. There, Washington's army, along with allied French troops, had cornered the British commander Lord Cornwallis. Cornwallis had been driven from his southern campaign by intense Patriot resistance. He had taken up refuge in a little tobacco port along the James River. From there, he intended to be rescued by an approaching British naval fleet. But, the fleet would never reach Cornwallis. A French fleet was blocking the approach to Chesapeake Bay, cutting off British access to its army stranded at Yorktown.

Hamilton took command of his new regiment by late September, when he arrived just a few miles outside Yorktown, Virginia. Excitement filled Washington's army as a great victory seemed to be certain. Hamilton was ordered to join his New York regiment with French troops under another of Washington's closest generals, a French volunteer, the Marquis de Lafayette. Together, their two forces numbered more than 16,000. The two armies began digging trenches toward the advance British positions. These trenches stretched on for more than one mile.

By mid-October, the men under the command of Hamilton and Lafayette were less than 350 yards from British forces situated in two small forts, called Redoubts 9 and 10. Four hundred men were chosen by Lafayette to make an assault on Redoubt 10, and Hamilton was selected to lead the charge. At last, Hamilton could engage in the combat he had wanted for years. On the clear, dark night of October 14, the Americans prepared for their assault. General Washington approached them on horseback, encouraging them to "act the part of firm and brave soldiers."[40] Their orders were to empty their rifles of all shot and powder. They were to advance quietly and surprise the enemy, using only their bayonets. (At the same time, the French forces were to advance and attack Redoubt 9.)

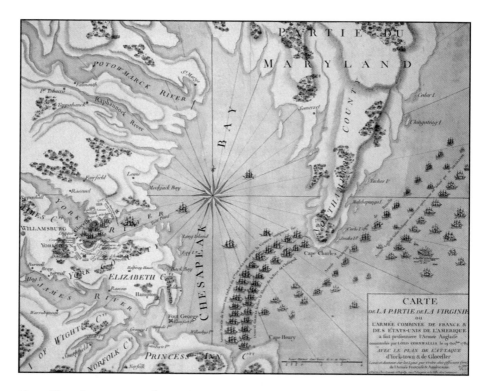

Hamilton's New York regiment joined forces with French troops under the command of the Marquis de Lafayette at Yorktown. British troops surrendered, marking the last, full-scale military engagement of the Revolutionary War. This French map illustrates how the British were defeated.

Hamilton led his forces out of their trench and charged across an open stretch of ground. Along the way, several of Hamilton's men fell and disappeared into unseen cannon craters. As hundreds of American soldiers ran a quarter of a mile across open terrain, their excited yells could be heard above the din of cannon fire. As one Hessian described the scene later, "They made such a terrible yell and loud cheering that one believed the whole wild hunt had broken out."[41] The young commander reached the parapet of Redoubt 10 ahead of his men. There, in the confusion of artillery explosions in the distance and British rockets lighting up the sky overhead, Hamilton leaped into the fort, where the British and Hessian forces, numbering about 60, soon surrendered. Hamilton and his men had attacked so quickly, the enemy had hardly had time to respond. As his men gathered in the captured fort, Hamilton was soon joined by his old comrade and former aide to Washington, John Laurens.

The attack was a small part of a larger victory. Five days later, Cornwallis surrendered his entire army. The Continental and French victory at Yorktown was complete, and the fighting of the Revolutionary War nearly over. It would be the last full-scale military engagement of the war. There would be many more skirmishes and limited sea battles before the war was negotiated to an end in 1783. But, for the moment, the Americans, with solid French support, had achieved victory over the British.

Even as the war ended, Hamilton's public career was beginning. Years later, he would look back on his assault on Redoubt 10 as the highlight of his experiences of 1780 and 1781. But the future, for Hamilton, would have more to do with his marriage to Betsey Schuyler than with his experiences in battle. By attaching himself to one of the richest and most politically powerful families in New York, Hamilton had paved the way for an exciting career that would include years of public service.

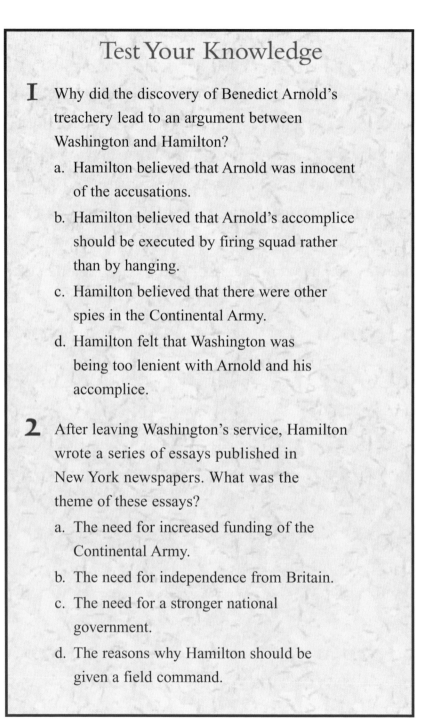

Test Your Knowledge

I Why did the discovery of Benedict Arnold's treachery lead to an argument between Washington and Hamilton?

   a. Hamilton believed that Arnold was innocent of the accusations.

   b. Hamilton believed that Arnold's accomplice should be executed by firing squad rather than by hanging.

   c. Hamilton believed that there were other spies in the Continental Army.

   d. Hamilton felt that Washington was being too lenient with Arnold and his accomplice.

2 After leaving Washington's service, Hamilton wrote a series of essays published in New York newspapers. What was the theme of these essays?

   a. The need for increased funding of the Continental Army.

   b. The need for independence from Britain.

   c. The need for a stronger national government.

   d. The reasons why Hamilton should be given a field command.

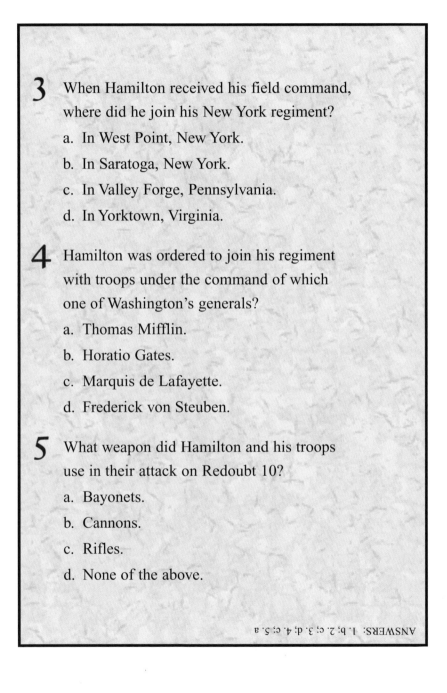

3   When Hamilton received his field command,
     where did he join his New York regiment?

     a. In West Point, New York.

     b. In Saratoga, New York.

     c. In Valley Forge, Pennsylvania.

     d. In Yorktown, Virginia.

4   Hamilton was ordered to join his regiment
     with troops under the command of which
     one of Washington's generals?

     a. Thomas Mifflin.

     b. Horatio Gates.

     c. Marquis de Lafayette.

     d. Frederick von Steuben.

5   What weapon did Hamilton and his troops
     use in their attack on Redoubt 10?

     a. Bayonets.

     b. Cannons.

     c. Rifles.

     d. None of the above.

ANSWERS: 1. b; 2. c; 3. d; 4. c; 5. a

OUR RIGHTS AND OUR LIBERTIES

8

Constitutional Reformer

A lexander Hamilton's future lay before him in 1782. This was certainly true at home. Within months of the Yorktown battle, Betsey Hamilton gave birth to a son, Philip, in January. Hamilton soon became a loving father who longed "for nothing but the company of my wife and my baby."[42] Before the war, Hamilton had been a college student. After the war, he decided to become a lawyer. During the spring months, Hamilton studied hard, reading legal documents and court cases. He met a fellow New Yorker who was a veteran of the war and also studying to become a lawyer—Aaron Burr. Their paths would remain linked until Hamilton's death, even if their friendship did not remain close. Although studying for the bar exam normally took five years to complete, Hamilton took the exam after only five months of study, passing with high marks in the summer of 1782.

Having become well known in New York for his service to Washington during the war, Hamilton was soon approached by members of the New York Assembly to serve in the Continental Congress. Ready to practice law, Hamilton refused at first, and then decided to take on the responsibility. He felt that he had a duty as an American citizen to serve his country in this important role.

When Hamilton joined the ranks of the Congress, he became a member of a new national government with many problems. The framework of government, the Articles of Confederation, did not give the national government much power. State power was often more important than national power. A general from New Hampshire, John Sullivan, described the Articles of Confederation government as "a Monster with Thirteen heads."[43] Among the most important problems facing the national government was the fact that the Articles allowed the Congress little ability to tax, leaving the legislature constantly short of funds. The military implications were clear. While Hamilton had resigned from military service following the Battle of Yorktown, Washington remained in the field with thousands of troops while the peace treaty between America and Great Britain was being negotiated. There was a continuing need for money for those troops.

In November 1782, a provisional peace treaty was signed between American and British representatives meeting in Paris. While this allowed Washington to begin dismantling his army and sending his troops home, the lack of money available to Congress continued. As the war officially ended (the peace treaty would not be official until 1783), the problems facing the Congress loomed large. Soldiers were beginning to demand back pay. Hamilton was sympathetic to them, and presented a proposal in Congress to provide five years' back pay for the Continental officers. But the move did not make the enlisted men happy. Members of the Pennsylvania State Militia soon surrounded the State House in Philadelphia where the Congress met. Rather than address the problem of back pay, the Congress packed up and moved to Princeton. These events deeply angered, frustrated, and disappointed Hamilton. It did not take long before Hamilton became so frustrated with serving in Congress that he asked to be replaced.

By July 1783, Hamilton had left Congress and returned to his family in Albany. Soon, he moved to New York City with Betsey and Philip, taking up residence at 57 Wall Street to begin his law career.

CALLS FOR REFORM

Hamilton was not ready to give up a role in directing the national government. He hoped that a stronger Congress and federal system of government could be established. A federal system would provide for a more powerful national government and weaker state governments. Hamilton talked to friends and influential politicians. While in Congress, he had met James Madison, a delegate from Virginia and fellow veteran of the Revolutionary War. Madison, too, wanted to see dramatic reform of the national government.

Little changed concerning the Articles of Confederation for the next several years. Hamilton continued to call for reform and a new constitution establishing a federal government. In the meantime, other events were directing his life. He helped establish the Bank of New York, which Hamilton promoted. He was appointed one of its directors in the spring of 1784. The following year, he helped establish an anti-slavery organization, the Society for the Manumission of Slaves. Hamilton had long been opposed to slavery and had supported the use of black troops in the Continental Army during the Revolution. In 1786, he called for an end to the American slave trade. Hamilton and his wife were also kept busy by their growing family. On September 25, 1784, Betsey gave birth to the first of Hamilton's daughters, named Angelica after Betsey's sister. Two years later, Betsey gave birth to a second son, Alexander Hamilton, Jr. The following year, the Hamiltons adopted a two-year-old girl, Fanny, whose parents had been friends of Alexander's. (The mother had died, and the father suffered a nervous breakdown.) In 1788, Elizabeth Hamilton delivered a fourth child, whom they named James Alexander. In all, the Hamiltons produced eight children over a 20-year period.

Hamilton worked as a lawyer, taking many cases and making lots of money. He handled cases involving simple contracts and wills, as well as criminal cases, including representing clients accused of murder. With each passing year, Hamilton's personal and professional star continued to rise.

At the same time, the government continued to govern poorly a nation that was quickly sinking into economic chaos. The money printed by the government was worthless, inflation was mounting, and the jails were filling with debtors unable to pay. Trade between the states went unregulated. Interest rates on many loans amounted to as much as 40 percent. States were also struggling. They, too, overprinted state money, which soon lost its value.

By the fall of 1786, Hamilton was named as a delegate to a convention called in Annapolis, Maryland. The convention was attended by delegates from five states, including New York, New Jersey, Pennsylvania, Delaware, and Virginia. The purpose of the meeting was to solve a problem the Articles of Confederation

Congress could not—trade regulations among the states, including the importation of foreign goods.

Hamilton desperately wanted to see a national import tax established. Since a minority of the states sent delegates to Annapolis, the meeting was doomed to failure. But those in attendance called for another convention for the following summer to discuss changing the Articles of Confederation. The decision excited Hamilton. Perhaps the changes he had been calling for could finally take place. He made his way to Philadelphia, arriving a week early, on May 18. He soon began meeting informally with several of the other delegates at the Indian Queen Tavern on Fourth Street. Hamilton was anxious to get to the business at hand.

THE CONSTITUTIONAL CONVENTION

When Hamilton took his seat at the Constitutional Convention in Philadelphia on May 25, 1787, he represented New York along with two other New Yorkers, Robert Yates and John Lansing, Jr. The delegates met in the same gray East Room of the Pennsylvania State House (today Independence Hall) where the Declaration of Independence had been signed 11 years earlier. All three of New York's representatives wanted to see the establishment of a strong federal government. Such a move would require the Articles to either be drastically changed or a completely new constitution to be written. The assembled delegates, once they all arrived, numbered 55, representing 12 of the 13 states. (Only Rhode Island chose to boycott the convention.)

Even before the first session, Hamilton began campaigning among his fellow delegates for a federal system to be adopted. One of his key contacts was James Madison from Virginia. Madison was prepared, also, to support a federal system. The Virginia political leader was so interested in what the convention might accomplish by creating a new framework of government that he had studied for months, reading from 200 books on subjects ranging from Greek democracy to philosophy to history. The meeting brought Washington and Hamilton back together, as Washington was soon selected as the president of the convention. He and Washington managed to renew their old friendship. These three men would play crucial roles at the convention. Historian Catharine Drinker Bowen credits them with bringing about the convention: "Among those who began early to work for reform three names stand out: Washington, Madison, and Hamilton. And of the three, evidence points to Hamilton as the most potent single influence toward calling the Convention of '87."[44]

Soon after the delegates began officially meeting, two plans were proposed that would bring serious change to the Articles of Confederation. James Madison proposed the Virginia Plan, which sought to establish a federal government with three branches: legislative (to make laws); executive (to enforce laws); and judicial (to interpret laws). The plan also called for a bicameral (two-house) congress, with membership based on the population of each state. Under this proposal, the states with larger populations would be allowed more representatives than smaller states.

In response, a delegate named William Paterson proposed the New Jersey Plan. This called for a unicameral (one-house) legislature, with equal representation for each state, regardless of size. He also called for a chief executive to enforce the laws and a Supreme Court. This plan met with instantaneous criticism since Rhode Island (population 68,000) would have as much power as Virginia (population 747,000).

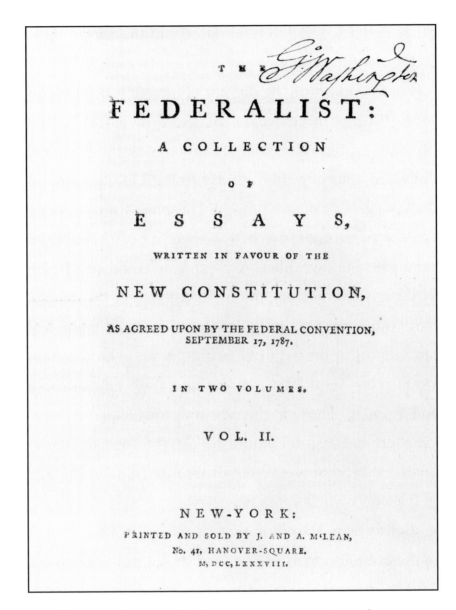

THE FEDERALIST:

A COLLECTION

OF

E S S A Y S,

WRITTEN IN FAVOUR OF THE

NEW CONSTITUTION,

AS AGREED UPON BY THE FEDERAL CONVENTION,
SEPTEMBER 17, 1787.

IN TWO VOLUMES.

VOL. II.

NEW-YORK:

PRINTED AND SOLD BY J. AND A. M'LEAN,
No. 41, HANOVER-SQUARE.
M, DCC, LXXXVIII.

Hamilton and James Madison were supporters of a new constitution for the United States. With John Jay, they anonymously published a series of essays outlining their ideas, known as *The Federalist Papers*. This copy contains George Washington's signature.

Such a plan seemed to retain power in the hands of the states, not the people.

As for Hamilton, he did not completely favor either plan. Within three weeks of the convention's first official session, Alexander Hamilton took the floor and delivered a speech. In his early thirties, he was one of the youngest delegates present. He spoke for five hours, largely from memory. In his long speech, Hamilton presented his own plan. A president would be chosen by designated electors, not by direct vote of the people. He would serve as president until he no longer had the support of the majority of the people. The congress would consist of two houses, including an assembly and a senate. Those in the assembly would serve three-year terms. Senators would be elected for life. Those qualified to vote would be all free males over the age of 21 who owned some property.

In this plan, Hamilton was revealing his lack of trust in the common man. He wanted to see political power held by the wealthy citizens with the best social standing and the best educations. Hamilton thought the upper class better suited for leadership. According to Hamilton: "The people are turbulent and changing; they seldom judge or determine right. Give, therefore, to the first class a distinct, permanent share in the government."[45] Hamilton had come to believe that all Americans would benefit if a government were established that favored those who created wealth, such as merchants, bankers, financial investors, creditors, and other prosperous individuals. In his speech, he also gave credit to the British and their form of government: "I have no scruple in declaring . . . that the British government is the best in the world."[46] Since many of the delegates believed England to be America's worst enemy, these words were shocking. Hamilton's proposal would never be accepted.

Test Your Knowledge

1 After the war, what profession did Hamilton choose?
a. Congressman.
b. Lawyer.
c. Doctor.
d. Journalist.

2 Which framework of government did Hamilton want to change or eliminate?
a. The Constitution.
b. The Bill of Rights.
c. The Articles of Confederation.
d. The presidency.

3 Which delegate from Virginia was actively involved in the plans for governmental reform?
a. James Madison.
b. James Monroe.
c. George Washington.
d. Thomas Jefferson.

4 Twelve of the thirteen states sent representatives to the Constitutional Convention. Which state boycotted the meeting?
a. Delaware.
b. Rhode Island.
c. New Jersey.
d. South Carolina.

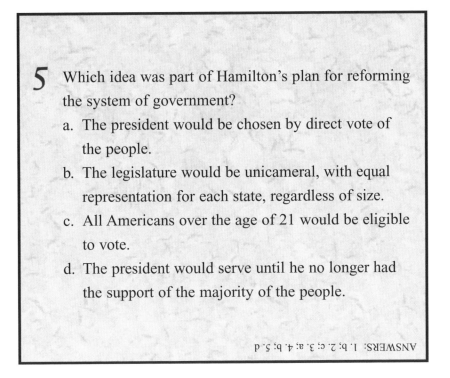

5 Which idea was part of Hamilton's plan for reforming the system of government?

a. The president would be chosen by direct vote of the people.

b. The legislature would be unicameral, with equal representation for each state, regardless of size.

c. All Americans over the age of 21 would be eligible to vote.

d. The president would serve until he no longer had the support of the majority of the people.

ANSWERS: 1. b; 2. c; 3. a; 4. b; 5. d

Directing the Nation's Economy

In the days that followed, Hamilton continued to work alongside other delegates as they hammered out a new framework of government. He met with Madison several times. Both men wanted to see senators serve as long as possible. They both represented more populous states and favored the Virginia Plan over the New Jersey Plan. But progress during the convention dragged on slowly. Surprisingly, just 11 days after delivering his five-hour speech, Hamilton chose to leave the convention. He had come to realize that his voice represented that of the minority of delegates. In addition, he was neglecting his law practice, as well as his family. However, even though he was not actively involved in the convention as a delegate after June 29, he remained extremely interested in its success.

Hamilton did return to his seat in September as the work of the convention was winding down. By then, a new constitution had been penned and a strong federal government was to be established in place of the weak national government under the Articles of Confederation. Those at the convention had finally compromised between the Virginia and New Jersey Plans. The "Great Compromise" established a House of Representatives (with membership based on state population), and a Senate (with every state represented by two senators). To give the House extra authority and power, it was decided that all money or tax bills would originate in that body. By other agreements, the delegates decided to create an executive branch with a president elected by an electoral college consisting of men chosen by local voters. The new constitution also established a national Supreme Court with power over all other courts. The new government would have the power to tax, regulate trade, and make treaties. And the federal government would be the highest power in the land, reducing the amount of power held by the states.

Fully based on compromise, the new constitution did not satisfy everyone. But, as Madison later admitted, "Great as the evil is, a dismemberment of the Union would be worse."[47] As for Hamilton, he was appointed to the Committee of Style, which was responsible for the specific wording of the new federal constitution. On September 17, the finished document was presented to the delegates. Just as the Declaration of Independence had been signed by the delegates of 1776, so Hamilton proposed that the delegates who supported this new constitution should also sign. Before delegates put their names on the document, Hamilton wrote in the names of each of the states.

THE FEDERALIST

Dozens of men from nearly all of the 13 states had spent a summer creating a new federal framework for the national government. But the fight was not over.

Many of the delegates were not entirely pleased with the proposed constitution. Most wondered if the document gave too much power to the federal government.

Hamilton was not one of them. Over the next six months—from October 27, 1787, through May 28, 1788—Hamilton, James Madison, and John Jay, an old friend who had served in the First Continental Congress (1774–1775)—published a series of more than 80 essays in support of the new constitution. They titled the essays *The Federalist Papers*. They did not sign their names to the essays, to avoid prejudice, but used the name "Publius." Hamilton wrote two-thirds of the essays, typically writing at night, while trying to maintain his law practice by day.

The Federalist Papers remain today an important set of essays on politics and the theory of government. In these essays, Hamilton and the others argued that the new constitution would establish a stronger, more stable government, a "more perfect union" of the states, as stated in the constitution's opening lines, called the Preamble. In the first of the essays, Hamilton wrote: "My Countrymen, I own to you, that, after having given it an attentive consideration, I am clearly of opinion, it is your interest to adopt [the new Constitution]. I am convinced, that this is the safest course for your liberty, your dignity, and your happiness."[48]

For his support of the new constitution, Hamilton was highly criticized, especially by his fellow New Yorkers. Leading the opposition was New York's Governor George Clinton, who did not want to surrender any of his state's power. Those who supported Hamilton and ratification, or acceptance, of the constitution became known as Federalists. Those who supported Clinton and wanted to see the constitution rejected were known as Anti-Federalists.

Hamilton fought tirelessly for ratification of the constitution. He wrote so much during the months following the convention that he only managed to sleep an average of five hours a night. He found himself in the middle of a statewide fight, with great opposition to the proposed document. Knowing New York would likely not ratify the constitution until other states had done so, he managed to postpone a vote until midsummer of 1788. By then, only three states had not voted for ratification, including New York, North Carolina, and Rhode Island.

On July 27, the New York convention was finally prepared to vote. Hamilton delivered a two-hour speech to the assembled state delegates present at the state capital at Poughkeepsie. In the speech, he described how the new constitution would create a "beautiful, wealthy, and happy United States."[49] Then, he described the misery and poverty that would befall New York if it did not agree to the federal document. When the vote was taken, the result was close—30 to 27 in favor of ratification. Alexander Hamilton would see his adopted state join a new federal republic of the United States of America.

Hamilton did not realize it at the time, but his support for the adoption of a new constitution and the creation of a new federal republic would change his life dramatically—and soon. Under the newly ratified constitution, a new president would be chosen to lead the executive branch of government. When the Electoral College met on February 4, 1789, they selected George Washington. On April 30, Washington was inaugurated. Determined to appoint a group of close advisors for his new presidency, Washington selected Alexander Hamilton to be his secretary of the treasury.

The role was perfect for Hamilton. For years, he had been interested in the national economy and how government could guide it for the benefit of the new nation and its people. Now, he would have his opportunity. To accept the government post, Hamilton agreed to a salary of $3,000 a year, much less than he usually made as a lawyer. But, once again, his desire to serve the public led him to accept Washington's appointment. In September 1789, the Senate approved Hamilton as the head of the federal treasury.

HAMILTONIAN ECONOMICS

Just as Washington created the office of the presidency by serving as the nation's first chief executive, so Hamilton was able to define the power of the role of secretary of the treasury. He went immediately to work to create a cabinet office of singular importance. Among the problems the young United States had been facing since the beginning of the Revolutionary War were questions swirling around money and government finances. Hamilton set the agenda for both. In part, he had support from the new Congress. Legislators encouraged him to develop an economic plan for the government in just three months. Hamilton would deliver.

He spent those months gathering facts and statistics on trade, tariffs, tax systems, money, and debt. Hamilton did not intend to tackle the American economy on his own. He began hiring assistants, training them for each of their roles and responsibilities. One at a time, he laid out an economic agenda to deal with each economic problem. One of the first focused on the nation's unstable currency. On January 4, 1790, he delivered to Congress a 40,000-word document titled *Report on Public Credit*. In this report, he described the United States as on the brink of bankruptcy, existing under a staggering $80 million debt owed to both Americans at home and investors abroad. Hamilton's solution for establishing a stable money system was for the national government to issue investment bonds. These government bonds could serve as backing for any bank notes (similar to paper money). Investors could buy such notes to develop their own business ventures, helping to expand the economy. The bonds would draw interest that, in the short run, would go to the government.

As for the existing debt, Hamilton insisted that the government pay it in full, not at a discounted rate of 50 cents or less on the dollar. If the national government did not honor its debts, as some were suggesting, it would lose face with both the American people and foreign investors and governments.

Another problem Hamilton faced was an argument over state debts. All the states had taken on debt during the American Revolution in helping to provide for their militia forces. Hamilton suggested that the federal government assume, or take over, those debts. The plan was controversial, especially in states that did not have a high war debt. They considered the plan unfair. Madison and others opposed this part of Hamilton's plan, claiming that it would create high federal taxes and promote antagonism between the states. But Hamilton argued that assumption would help establish not only the power of the federal government, but would help shore up the ailing economies of the states.

As he had always believed, Hamilton also stated in his report that the federal government should provide the back pay and other promises made to Continental soldiers during the Revolutionary War. All these suggestions by the secretary of the treasury were controversial. For nearly two weeks, Congress debated the merits of the report. Then, on April 12, 1790, Congress voted on the assumption issue, defeating it by a vote of 29 to 31.

Hamilton did not give up. He met with a fellow cabinet member, Secretary of State Thomas Jefferson.

Thomas Jefferson (pictured above) served with Hamilton in George Washington's first cabinet, Jefferson as secretary of state and Hamilton as secretary of the treasury. The two strongly disagreed on the direction for the new country, and would later become the leaders of the first two American political parties.

Jefferson and Hamilton did not agree on the specifics of Hamilton's economic plan or even on the question of how much power the federal government should have at the expense of the states. Jefferson, like Madison, wanted to see the states retain much of their power, even as a federal government replaced the weak government under the Articles of Confederation. During Washington's first term as president, the two men became the leaders of the first political parties in United States history: the Federalists, led by Hamilton, and the Anti-Federalists (or Democratic Republicans), led by Jefferson. (By 1792, the two parties were clearly drawn.)

When the two men sat down and shared a dinner, Hamilton asked for Jefferson's support for assumption. The Virginian agreed to help sway southern votes toward Hamilton's plan only after Hamilton agreed to support moving the federal capital to Virginia, Jefferson's home state. (By 1800, the capital was, indeed, moved south, but to Maryland, just across the Potomac River from Virginia.)

In July, Congress voted again on the assumption question, this time passing the measure by a vote of 34 to 28. Hamilton had won a crucial victory for his economic plan. But assumption met with violent criticism, nearly all of which was pointed at Hamilton. Critics believed assumption took away state power and increased the power of the national government. For the most part, the assumption issue drove Madison away from future support of Hamilton.

Hamilton was quickly becoming a controversial figure on the national scene. That December, he proposed another plan, presenting his *Report on a National Bank* to Congress. He had made a similar proposal more than ten years earlier. Hamilton's plan called for a national bank in which the government would own 20 percent of the stock. The remaining 80 percent would be funded and owned by private investors willing to put their money into the bank. Hamilton believed that only the wealthy could provide enough funds to float his national bank idea. Others said that such a bank would only profit the rich. While controversial, Congress voted in favor of establishing a national bank in February 1791, by a vote of 39 to 20.

The previous month, Hamilton had proposed the establishment of a national mint for producing gold and silver coins. While Jefferson and Hamilton argued heavily on this issue (Hamilton's proposal would deny

Hamilton proposed the creation of a national bank in which the government would own 20 percent of the stock. Congress voted to support the controversial plan in February 1791.

the states the power to mint and print coins and paper money), the proposal passed in Congress. Hamilton's plan helped establish a coin system that included the copper half-cent, the cent, a ten-cent piece, a silver dollar, a gold dollar, and a $10 gold coin.

Hamilton also created a system for raising revenue for the federal government. He called for the establishment of a national duty, or tax, of 25 cents per gallon on alcohol produced domestically. The bill passed in March 1791. Although frontiersmen and farmers who produced their own alcohol protested the so-called Whiskey Tax, the tax was collected. When western Pennsylvania producers rallied against the tax, Washington ordered militia troops sent in to put down the rebellion.

In November, Hamilton issued yet another economic study, his *Report on the Subject of Manufactures*. In this report, he argued in favor of government support of the developing manufacturing sector. Few factories existed in America, and Hamilton believed that America's future would center on a well-developed industrial base. Again, Jefferson, who wanted to see an America of farmer-citizens, expressed opposition. Once again, a policy change proposed by Hamilton generated controversy.

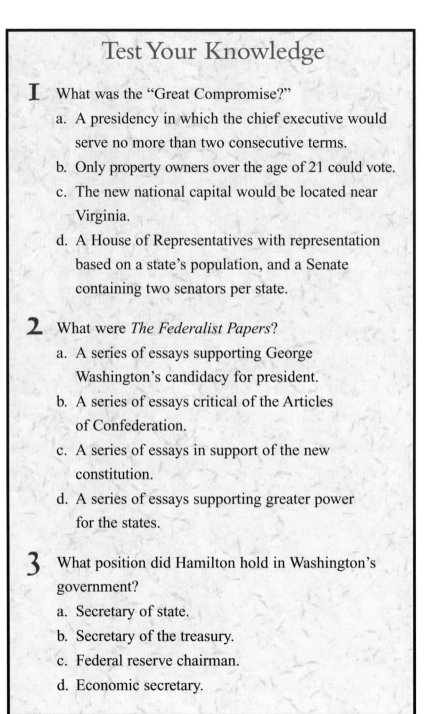

Test Your Knowledge

I What was the "Great Compromise?"

   a. A presidency in which the chief executive would serve no more than two consecutive terms.

   b. Only property owners over the age of 21 could vote.

   c. The new national capital would be located near Virginia.

   d. A House of Representatives with representation based on a state's population, and a Senate containing two senators per state.

2 What were *The Federalist Papers*?

   a. A series of essays supporting George Washington's candidacy for president.

   b. A series of essays critical of the Articles of Confederation.

   c. A series of essays in support of the new constitution.

   d. A series of essays supporting greater power for the states.

3 What position did Hamilton hold in Washington's government?

   a. Secretary of state.

   b. Secretary of the treasury.

   c. Federal reserve chairman.

   d. Economic secretary.

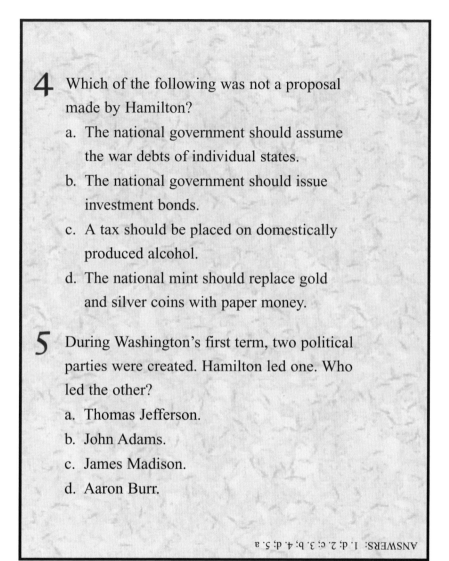

4 Which of the following was not a proposal made by Hamilton?

a. The national government should assume the war debts of individual states.

b. The national government should issue investment bonds.

c. A tax should be placed on domestically produced alcohol.

d. The national mint should replace gold and silver coins with paper money.

5 During Washington's first term, two political parties were created. Hamilton led one. Who led the other?

a. Thomas Jefferson.

b. John Adams.

c. James Madison.

d. Aaron Burr.

ANSWERS: 1. d; 2. c; 3. b; 4. d; 5. a

OUR RIGHTS AND OUR LIBERTIES

"Mine Is an Odd Destiny"

While Hamilton's policies were themselves controversial, his private life soon became controversial, as well. Hamilton had always engaged in an active family life, since his wife and children meant a great deal to him. But he had also developed a reputation as a ladies' man. During the summer of 1791, he became involved in a relationship with a married woman, Maria (pronounced Mariah) Reynolds. Mrs. Reynolds claimed that her husband, James Reynolds, had abandoned her. On several occasions, Hamilton gave her money and, while his family was away, he began spending time with her. By summer's end, Hamilton was ready to end the relationship, and then her husband threatened to publicly embarrass Hamilton. Only then did Hamilton realize he had been duped into the relationship by the scheming couple, who threatened to blackmail Hamilton.

James Reynolds asked Hamilton for a clerk's position at the Treasury Department. Hamilton refused. Reynolds demanded money to keep quiet about the relationship. Hamilton paid him $1,000. Then, Reynolds asked for more money. Hamilton kept paying, hoping that the scandal would not break, that his reputation would not be damaged, and that his wife would not learn of his indiscretions. However, the Reynolds affair did become common knowledge.

Soon, members of Congress began to turn against Hamilton. He lost support for portions of his economic plan. By early 1793, the House of Representatives voted to impeach Hamilton. The charges against him included immoral and unethical behavior in office, including questionable bookkeeping methods. Although the House voted down the accusations in March, Hamilton knew that his reputation as a member of Washington's cabinet was destroyed. Through 1794, he continued to write economic reports and campaign for his theories of effective government. But his effectiveness as secretary of the treasury had slipped away. He was facing personal financial difficulties and poor health, as well. By January of 1795, he resigned his position. Ironically, Jefferson had also resigned, leaving his post as secretary of state more than a year earlier.

LIFE AS A PRIVATE CITIZEN

Out of public office, Hamilton returned to New York City, where he took up his law practice. He was one of the most popular, well-known attorneys in the city. Although he had resigned from the national government, Hamilton still offered advice to Washington and members of Congress, even when they did not ask for it. When Washington was near the end of his second term as president in

1796, Hamilton wrote one of the drafts of his farewell speech.

Hamilton considered running for the presidency in 1796, but was bypassed by the Federalists, who supported Vice President John Adams, instead. The opposition party, the Democrat-Republicans, ran two candidates: Thomas Jefferson and Aaron Burr. Hamilton did not like either. Although he was no fan of John Adams, he did campaign on his behalf as a fellow Federalist. The election brought Adams to the presidency with Jefferson as his vice president. (At this time, the candidate, regardless of party, who received the largest number of electoral votes became president, and the candidate receiving the second largest number became vice president.)

Hamilton continued to dabble in politics, both state and national. When a clash developed between the American government and the French over the illegal seizure of American merchant ships, Washington was called out of retirement to lead an American army, and Hamilton was selected as his second-in-command. It appeared that the two former comrades-at-arms might fight side by side once again. But the war never materialized.

In 1799, Hamilton experienced two great tragedies. That year, both his father and George Washington died. Of Washington's death, Hamilton told a colleague: "Perhaps no friend of his has more cause to lament on personal account then myself!"[50] That same year, the Hamiltons experienced the joy of yet another birth, a daughter named Eliza.

Hamilton took a leading role in the election of 1800, which once again pitted Jefferson and Adams opposite one another. Hamilton rallied and supported his fellow Federalists, especially in New York. However, Republicans swept the election, winning a majority in Congress and the presidency. But the presidential vote soon hit a snag. When the electoral votes were counted, both Republican candidates— Jefferson and Burr—received the same number. The vote was a tie. The election was to be decided in the House of Representatives. While Burr had run hoping to gain the vice presidency, he suddenly found the possibility of becoming president within his grasp. The vote in the Congress was as tight as the Electoral College vote had been. After 36 ballots in six days, Jefferson was finally elected president and Burr became vice president.

During Jefferson's presidency, Hamilton was a constant opponent. He wrote 18 essays criticizing his former cabinet colleague. But Hamilton's voice had changed. His accusations and finger-pointing seemed less political and more personal. Perhaps Hamilton understood that his days of effective political power had passed. Republicans seemed poised to lead America into the nineteenth century.

A REDIRECTED LIFE

With Jefferson's election, Hamilton began to fade from public view. The Federalist Party was quickly dying and the nation appeared ready to follow paths Hamilton did not appreciate. In 1802, after much of his public life was behind him and with Thomas Jefferson solidly in the presidency, Hamilton observed of himself:

> Mine is an odd destiny. Perhaps no man in the United States has sacrificed or done more for the present constitution than myself; and contrary to all my anticipations of its fate . . . from the very beginning, I am still laboring to prop the frail and worthless fabric, yet I have the murmurs of its

(continued on page 130)

Like Father, Like Son

The final years of Hamilton's life were marked by both success and tragedy. In 1801, five years before his death, Alexander Hamilton experienced one of the greatest emotional losses of his life, the death of his 19-year-old son, Philip.

Philip was a bright young man, but he had an undisciplined side, which eventually landed him in trouble. In late November 1801, Philip attended the Park Theater in Manhattan to see a comedy. In the theater, he spotted a Republican rival and critic of his father, George Eacker. With a companion, Philip broke into the theater box where Eacker was seated with three friends, and began taunting him. Eacker at first ignored the young men, then asked Philip Hamilton to join him in the lobby. There, Eacker said, "It is abominable to be publicly insulted by a set of rascals."* At that time, the word "rascal" was used as an insult that often led to a duel. The two men exchanged insults until an angered Eacker grabbed Hamilton by the collar. While the two broke off their scuffle, Hamilton's friend, a young man named Price, challenged Eacker to a duel. Eacker agreed.

Two days later, the two young men—Eacker and Price—dueled, firing a total of four shots with no injury to either man. The matter was considered settled. Eacker also had challenged Hamilton to a duel, and this was set for the following day at 3:00 P.M. Hamilton arranged the duel with Eacker without his father's knowledge. When the elder Hamilton did learn of the planned duel, he advised his son to allow Eacker to fire first, then fire off his own pistol in the air. But the plan did not go well. As the duel unfolded, Eacker shot and hit Hamilton, the ball striking above his right hip, jagging through his body, and lodging in his left arm. Hamilton's pistol then went off accidentally. The duel was ended, and young Hamilton rushed to a doctor. By 5:00 A.M. the following day, Hamilton had died of his wounds.

His parents were emotionally crushed. His mother was three months pregnant and devastated by the event, as was her husband. When Hamilton's sister, Angelica, learned of his death, she experienced a mental breakdown and fell into insanity. The family went into mourning. Six months later, Elizabeth Hamilton delivered her baby, who was christened Philip.

* Ron Chernow, *Alexander Hamilton* (New York: Penguin Press, 2004), 652.

(continued from page 127)

friends no less than the curses of its foes for my reward. What can I do better than withdraw from the scene? Every day proves to me more and more that the American world was not made for me.[51]

Hamilton began to content himself with his law practice, his family, and the completion of his estate, The Grange, which he had had built nestled in the New York countryside. He enjoyed the company of his children and spent much time teaching them songs that he had learned as a soldier in the Revolutionary War. He took up gardening, and became especially found of raising flowers, including tulips, hyacinths, lilies, and roses. As a fellow Federalist noted of Hamilton in 1803: "I don't perceive that he meddles or feels much concerning politics."[52]

He had not given up politics completely, however, and still tried to drum up support for the Federalist Party. He spoke out frequently against Vice President Aaron Burr. In 1804, Burr decided to run for the governorship of New York. Opposed to Burr's candidacy, Hamilton published articles criticizing him. Hamilton accused Burr of being motivated by personal ambition and desire for political power. After Burr lost the election by a vote of 22,000 to nearly 31,000, he partially blamed Hamilton for his loss. The two men were soon headed toward a showdown.

After losing the election, Burr cited a newspaper clipping in which Hamilton was quoted saying of the former vice president: "Mr Burr [was] a dangerous man, and one who ought not to be trusted with the reins of government."[53] Burr demanded that Hamilton retract his words. Hamilton refused.

After exchanging threats and accusations, Burr finally challenged Hamilton to a duel on June 27, 1804. Hamilton accepted, and the duel date was set for July 11, on the New Jersey side of the Hudson River at Weehawken. (Dueling was, then, illegal in New York.)

THE DUEL

As the day of the duel approached, Hamilton told a handful of friends that he did not intend to try and kill Burr: "I have resolved . . . to reserve and throw away my first fire, and I have thoughts even of reserving my second fire—and thus giving a double opportunity to Col. Burr to pause and to reflect."[54] Uncertain what the results would be, Hamilton made out his will. Should

Former Vice President Aaron Burr blamed Hamilton for his
defeat in his campaign to serve as governor of New York. Burr
challenged Hamilton to a duel, which was held on July 11, 1804.

he die, he would leave behind a wife and seven children
ranging in age from two to twenty. He wrote a note to
Elizabeth, which she would not see until after the duel:

This letter, my very dear Eliza, will not be delivered
to you, unless I shall first have terminated my earthly
career; to begin, as I humbly hope from redeeming

grace and divine mercy, a happy immortality. . . . Fly to the bosom of your God and be comforted. With my last idea, I shall cherish the sweet hope of meeting you in a better world. Adieu best of wives and best of women. Embrace all my darling Children for me. Ever yours AH[55]

At 5:00 A.M. on July 11, 1804, Hamilton and his second crossed the Hudson River to Weehawken. By 7:00 A.M., the duelists, their seconds, and a few friends (including a doctor) were present. Hamilton and Burr stepped off ten paces. The men examined their pistols and waited until one of their seconds shouted the signal: "Present!" By the rules of dueling, either man was then free to fire at the other. Both men raised their single-shot dueling pistols and, despite Hamilton's original intention to hold back his first shot, both pistols fired.

Hamilton felt a pain in his right side, rose up on his toes, and immediately fell to the ground. Burr was unwounded, and immediately broke off the duel. The pistol shot had broken one of Hamilton's ribs, struck his liver, and lodged in his spine. In great pain, he claimed he had not intended to fire. Hamilton was then taken to a house across the river in New York, where he suffered for the next 31 hours. He finally died at 2:00 P.M. the following day, his wife and children at his side.

Across the state, New Yorkers went into mourning. Much of the rest of the country grieved at the tragic loss of one of America's Founding Fathers. He was buried in the yard of Trinity Church in New York City. Hamilton was only 49 years old.

LEGACY OF A LEADER

Today, Alexander Hamilton is remembered as one of the most important guiding voices of the American republic he helped create in the long, hot summer of 1789. During his successful life, he experienced the American dream, enjoying a place of opportunity; a land where talent and intent, personal ambition and drive allowed an orphaned immigrant to become an important American leader. Through his public service as soldier, essayist, political thinker, and the nation's first treasurer, Hamilton gave his adopted country his best.

Hamilton's home, The Grange, still stands today on a bluff overlooking the Hudson River, just off New York's 145th Street, on the upper end of Manhattan.

It is fitting that Alexander Hamilton, who had focused on the creation of a strong economy for the United States, is honored with his picture on the ten-dollar bill.

A few years before his death, Hamilton had planted 13 trees at The Grange, symbolizing the 13 colonies for whom he had fought to gain their independence. Those trees still stand today, a testament of Hamilton's love of patriotism and the hope symbolized by America. In a similar way, through his life, Alexander Hamilton's love of country grew as he grew, took root, and never withered.

Test Your Knowledge

I What did Hamilton do after leaving his position as secretary of the treasury?
   a. He returned to his law practice.
   b. He ran for the governorship of New York.
   c. He began teaching classes in politics.
   d. He traveled to France.

2 Hamilton considered running for the presidency in 1796, but the Federalist Party selected another candidate. Who was it?
   a. Thomas Jefferson.
   b. Aaron Burr.
   c. John Adams.
   d. James Madison.

3 When America and France clashed over the illegal seizure of American merchant ships, Hamilton was asked to serve in what position?
   a. As secretary of defense.
   b. As ambassador to France.
   c. As second-in-command to George Washington in the war that was expected to result from the conflict.
   d. As commander-in-chief of the American military.

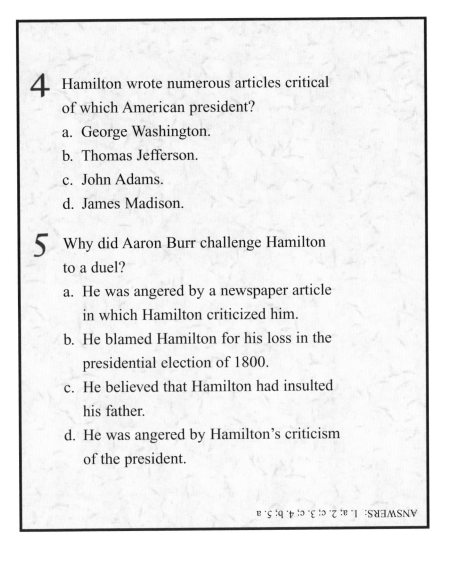

4 Hamilton wrote numerous articles critical
of which American president?

a. George Washington.

b. Thomas Jefferson.

c. John Adams.

d. James Madison.

5 Why did Aaron Burr challenge Hamilton
to a duel?

a. He was angered by a newspaper article
in which Hamilton criticized him.

b. He blamed Hamilton for his loss in the
presidential election of 1800.

c. He believed that Hamilton had insulted
his father.

d. He was angered by Hamilton's criticism
of the president.

ANSWERS: 1. a; 2. c; 3. c; 4. b; 5. a

1755 Hamilton is born on the Caribbean island of Nevis.

1765 Hamilton's father abandons his common-law wife, Rachel, and their two sons.

1768 Hamilton's mother dies of yellow fever; he is apprenticed to Nicholas Cruger, a New York merchant.

1772 Violent hurricane hits St. Croix.

1773 Supporters send Hamilton to America to get a formal education; he enrolls at Elizabethtown Academy in New Jersey.

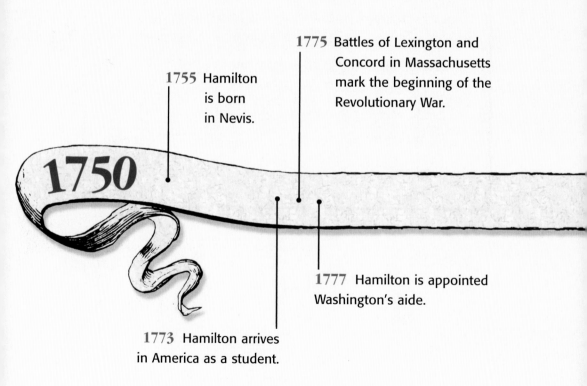

1755 Hamilton is born in Nevis.

1775 Battles of Lexington and Concord in Massachusetts mark the beginning of the Revolutionary War.

1750

1777 Hamilton is appointed Washington's aide.

1773 Hamilton arrives in America as a student.

1774   After being rejected admission by Princeton officials, Hamilton enrolls in King's College in New York.

1775   Hamilton and several other students create a volunteer fighting unit called the "Corsicans"; they remove cannon from nearby Fort George before the British can capture them.

1776   New York legislature forms an artillery company that Hamilton commands. Hamilton participates in the struggle to hold New York City; during this conflict, he meets Aaron Burr. In December, Hamilton's artillery unit participates in Washington's

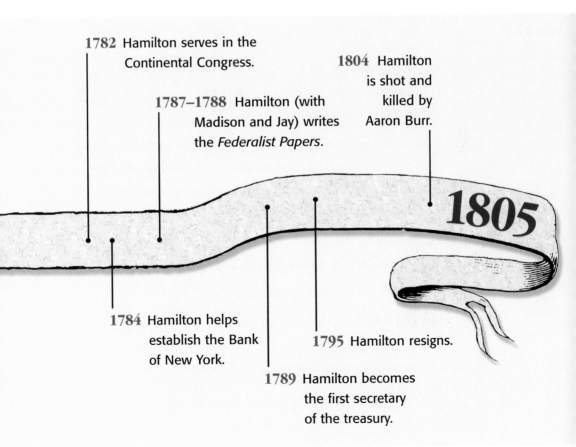

1782 Hamilton serves in the Continental Congress.

1787–1788 Hamilton (with Madison and Jay) writes the *Federalist Papers*.

1804 Hamilton is shot and killed by Aaron Burr.

1805

1784 Hamilton helps establish the Bank of New York.

1795 Hamilton resigns.

1789 Hamilton becomes the first secretary of the treasury.

surprise attack on the Hessian garrison at Trenton, New Jersey.

1777 Hamilton's artillery unit is part of the battle of Princeton; Washington appoints him as an aide-de-camp, with the rank of lieutenant colonel.

1778 Hamilton participates in the battle of Monmouth, during which his horse is shot out from under him.

1779 In the midst of the Revolutionary War, Hamilton begins promoting the idea of a national bank for the new United States.

1780 Hamilton falls in love with Elizabeth Schuyler; they marry in December.

1781 Hamilton resigns as Washington's aide; writes a series of articles calling for a strong national government. Hamilton is given field command, and participates in the Battle of Yorktown.

1782 Elizabeth Hamilton gives birth to the first of their eight children, Philip. Hamilton passes the bar exam, and is approached by New York politicians to serve in the Continental Congress.

1783 Frustrated by the inability of the government to bring about change, Hamilton resigns his seat.

1784 Hamilton helps establish the Bank of New York.

1787 Hamilton attends the Constitutional Convention; he makes significant contributions to the establishment of a new constitution that supports a strong national government.

Chronology

1787–1788 Hamilton, with James Madison and John Jay, pens the *Federalist Papers*.

1789 Hamilton is named the country's first secretary of the treasury.

1793 The House of Representatives votes to impeach Hamilton; Congressmen vote down the accusations.

1795 Hamilton resigns from his role as secretary of the treasury.

1796 After considering running for the presidency as a Federalist, Hamilton is passed over by the party in favor of John Adams.

1799 George Washington and Hamilton's father die.

1800 Hamilton supports the Federalist candidate, John Adams, for president, but Adams loses.

1804 Hamilton publicly criticizes Aaron Burr during Burr's campaign for governor of New York. Burr challenges Hamilton to a duel. Hamilton is shot, and dies on July 12.

Notes

CHAPTER 1
Caribbean Beginnings
1 Quoted in Ron Chernow, *Alexander Hamilton* (New York: Penguin Press, 2004), 13.
2 Ibid.
3 Quoted in Broadus Mitchell, *Heritage from Hamilton* (New York: Columbia University Press, 1957), 3.
4 Quoted in Mary-Jo Kline, ed. *Alexander Hamilton: A Biography in His Own Words,* Volume I (New York: Newsweek, 1973), 15.
5 Quoted in Chernow, 22.
6 Ibid., 26.

CHAPTER 2
A Brilliant Young Man
7 Ibid., 30.
8 Ibid., 31.
9 Ibid., 36.
10 Ibid.
11 Quoted in Alexander Hamilton, *Writings* (New York: The Library of America, 2001), 6.
12 Ibid., 7

CHAPTER 3
Patriot Origins
13 Quoted in Chernow, 43.
14 Ibid., 43.
15 Ibid.
16 Ibid., 44.
17 Quoted in James Thomas Flexner, *The Young Hamilton, A Biography* (Boston: Little, Brown and Company, 1978), 64.

18 Quoted in Nathan Schachner, *Alexander Hamilton* (New York: Thomas Yoseloff, 1957), 32.
19 Ibid.
20 Quoted in Chernow, 55.

CHAPTER 4
The Approach of Revolution
21 Ibid., 58.
22 Ibid.
23 Quoted in Hamilton, 11–12.
24 Ibid., 42.
25 Ibid., 43.
26 Quoted in Flexner, p. 77.
27 Ibid.
28 Ibid.,123.

CHAPTER 5
Through the Ranks
29 Ibid., 127.
30 Ibid.
31 Ibid., 128.
32 Quoted in Schachner, 54.
33 Quoted in Anne Erskine Crouse, *Alexander Hamilton and Aaron Burr: Their Lives, Their Times, Their Duel* (New York: Random House, 1958), 54.

CHAPTER 6
Love and Separation
34 Quoted in Chernow, 90.
35 Quoted in Nancy Whitelaw, *More Perfect Union: The Story of Alexander Hamilton* (Greensboro, N.C.: Morgan Reynolds Publishing, Inc., 2003), 32.
36 Quoted in Chernow, 129.

37 Ibid., 130–31.

38 Quoted in Hamilton, 79.

CHAPTER 7
Love and War

39 Quoted in Whitelaw, 39.

40 Quoted in Flexner, 363.

41 Quoted in Chernow, 163.

CHAPTER 8
Constitutional Reformer

42 Hamilton, 115.

43 Quoted in John Ferling, *A Leap in the Dark: The Struggle to Create the American Republic* (New York: Oxford University Press, 2003), 235.

44 Quoted in Catherine Drinker Bowen, *Miracle at Philadelphia: The Story of the Constitutional Convention, May to September 1787* (Boston: Little, Brown and Company, 1966), 5.

45 Quoted in Schachner, 200.

46 Quoted in Whitelaw, 56.

CHAPTER 9
Directing the Nation's Economy

47 Quoted in Tim McNeese, *The Revolutionary War* (St. Louis: Milliken, 2003), 31.

48 Quoted in Hamilton, 185.

49 Quoted in Whitelaw, 67.

CHAPTER 10
"Mine Is an Odd Destiny"

50 Ibid.,101.

51 Quoted in Flexner, 451.

52 Quoted in Hamilton, 665.

53 Quoted in Whitelaw, 108.

54 Ibid.,109.

55 Ibid.,110.

Bibliography

Bowen, Catherine Drinker. *Miracle at Philadelphia: The Story of the Constitutional Convention, May to September 1787*. Boston: Little, Brown and Company, 1966.

Chernow, Ron. *Alexander Hamilton*. New York: Penguin Press, 2004.

Crouse, Anna Erskine. *Alexander Hamilton and Aaron Burr: Their Lives, Their Times, Their Duel*. New York: Random House, 1958.

Ferling, John. *A Leap in the Dark: The Struggle to Create the American Republic*. New York: Oxford University Press, 2003.

Flexner, James Thomas. *The Young Hamilton, A Biography*. Boston: Little, Brown and Company, 1978.

Hamilton, Alexander. *Writings*. New York: The Library of America, 2001.

Kline, Mary-Jo, ed. *Alexander Hamilton: A Biography in His Own Words*, Vols. I and II. New York: Newsweek, 1973.

McDowell, Bart. *The Revolutionary War*. Washington, D.C.: National Geographic Society, 1967.

McNeese, Tim. *The Revolutionary War*. St. Louis: Milliken Publishing, 2003.

Mee, Charles L. *The Genius of the People*. New York: Harper & Row Publishers, 1987.

Mitchell, Broadus. *Heritage from Hamilton*. New York: Columbia University Press, 1957.

Schachner, Nathan. *Alexander Hamilton*. New York: Thomas Yoseloff, 1957.

Whitelaw, Nancy. *More Perfect Union: The Story of Alexander Hamilton*. Greensboro, N.C.: Morgan Reynolds Publishing, Inc., 2003.

Further Reading

Collier, James Lincoln. *The Alexander Hamilton You Never Knew*. New York: Scholastic Library Publishing, 2004.

Egan, Tracie, ed. *Alexander Hamilton: American Statesman*. New York: Rosen Publishing Group, Inc., 2003.

Haugen, Brenda and Andrew Santella. *Alexander Hamilton*. Minneapolis, Minn.: Compass Point Books, 2005.

Jones, Veda Boyd. *Alexander Hamilton*. Philadelphia: Chelsea House Publishers, 1999.

Kallen, Stuart A. *Alexander Hamilton*. Edina, Minn.: ABDO Publishing Company, 2001.

Keller, Mollie, and Richard Brandon Morris. *Alexander Hamilton*. Danbury, Conn.: Franklin Watts, 1986.

Kurland, Gerald. *Alexander Hamilton: Architect of American Nationalism*. Charlottesville, N.Y.: SamHar Press, 1972.

Levy, Elizabeth, and Daniel McFeeley. *Revolting Revolutionaries, 1750s–1790*. New York: Scholastic, Inc., 2003.

McLeese, Don. *Alexander Hamilton*. Vero Beach, Fla.: Rourke Publishing, 2004.

Rosenberg, Pam. *Alexander Hamilton*. Eden Prairie, Minn.: Child's World, 2004.

WEBSITES

Colonial Hall Biography
http://www.colonialhall.com/hamilton/hamilton.php

Historic Valley Forge
www.ushistory.org/valleyforge/served/hamilton.html

New York Historical Society
www.alexanderhamiltonexhibition.org

Rise and Fall of Alexander Hamilton
http://xroads.virginia.edu/~CAP/ham/hampltcs.html

Index

Adams, John
politics, 125–26, 136–37, 141
Adams, Samuel, 2, 32, 36
America
colonies, 2, 14, 19, 21, 23, 26,
28, 31–32, 38, 41, 69
patriot movement, 27, 37–41, 49,
52, 58, 65, 85, 87, 90
politics, 25, 29–32, 34, 39–41
and taxes, 2, 28, 31, 35
American Revolutionary war
after, 96, 112, 114
battles of, 2, 41, 43–44, 47,
49–50, 55, 60–65, 67–68,
70–73, 77–78, 85–88, 138–40
leaders of, 2–3, 32–33, 66, 69,
80, 82
Andre, John, 80
Anti-Federalists. *See* Democratic
Republicans
Arnold, Benedict, 80, 90
Articles of Confederation, 74, 80
problems with, 93–94, 96–100,
104, 107, 116 120
Asia (British warship), 46, 52

Barber, Francis, 26
Beekman, David, 16, 20
Boston
Hamilton in, 24–25, 35
politics, 25, 33, 35, 41–43, 49
Boston Tea Party, 31–33
Boudinot, Elias, 27–28, 31
Bowen, Catharine Drinker, 99
Bunker Hill, Battle of, 43, 56
Burgoyne, Johnny, 71
Burr, Aaron, 55, 57
duel with Hamilton, 55, 82,
131–34, 137, 139, 141
politics, 125–26, 130–31, 136

Burr, Aaron, Sr., 14, 25, 93

Clinton, George, 110
Committee of Style, 108
Concord, Battle of, 2, 41, 44, 138
Constitutional Convention
adoption, 111–12
creation, 3, 74, 96, 98
Hamilton as member, 98–104,
106–11, 140
Continental Army, 3
leaders of, 42–43, 46–53, 55, 59,
61–63, 72, 79, 81–82, 87, 90,
94–96
Continental Congress
Hamilton as member, 93–95,
109, 139–40
members, 38, 47, 67, 70–72, 77,
79, 81, 84, 98, 102, 109, 140
"Continentalist, The," 84
Cooper, Myles, 44–45
Cornwallis, Charles, 50, 64, 85, 88
Corsicans, 42, 52, 139
Cruger, Nicholas
Hamilton's master, 10, 14, 16,
18, 20, 22, 24–25, 27, 138

Declaration of Independence, 2,
49, 98, 108
"Defense of the Destruction of the
Tea," 32–33
Democratic Republicans (Anti-
Federalists)
establishment, 110, 116
members, 125–28
Dickinson, John, 2

Eacker, George, 128–29
Elizabethtown Academy
Hamilton at, 26, 138

Federalist Papers
  writers of, 101, 109–12, 120,
    139, 141
Federalist party, 101, 141
  establishment, 110, 116
  members, 125–27, 130, 136
France, 125, 136
  ally of Americans, 72, 77, 85–88

Gates, Horatio, 71, 73, 91
George, Fort, 52, 139
George II, King of England, 65, 68
George III, King of England, 31,
  68
Grange, The (home), 130, 134–35
Great Britain, 16, 58
  government, 2, 31, 33, 37–39,
    103
  loyalists, 24–25, 37–41, 44
  struggle with the colonies, 23,
    25, 28, 33, 49, 90
  troops, 25, 36, 41–41, 46, 51,
    53–54, 56, 63–64, 67–68,
    70–72, 77, 85–88, 94
Great Compromise, 107–8, 120

Hamilton, Alexander
  aide to Washington, 43, 65–66,
    68–84, 138, 140
  apprenticeship, 10, 12–16, 18,
    22, 138
  birth, 6, 11, 17–18, 138
  childhood, 7–15, 17–20
  chronology and timeline, 138–41
  critics and controversy, 117, 119,
    122–24
  death, 93, 128, 134–35, 139, 141
  duel with Burr, 55, 82, 131–34,
    137, 141
  economics, 112–21, 123–24 135

education, 8, 14–16, 20–31,
  33–35, 41–42, 46–47, 93,
  138–39
marriage, 46, 75, 79, 81, 84, 89,
  140
military career, 2, 42–53, 55,
  57–66, 68–94, 125, 136,
  139–40
political career, 2–6, 29, 31–34,
  36–41, 47, 52, 89, 91, 93–127,
  130, 136, 139–41
vision of America's future, 3–5,
  74, 84, 93–108, 114–17
Hamilton, Alexander, Jr. (son), 96
Hamilton, Angelica (daughter), 96,
  129
Hamilton, Eliza (daughter), 126
Hamilton, Elizabeth Schuyler
  (wife), 29–30, 73, 76, 78, 95, 132
  children, 92, 96–97, 129
  marriage, 46, 75, 79, 81, 89, 140
Hamilton, Fanny (daughter), 96
Hamilton, James (brother), 7–8,
  10
Hamilton, James (father), 6–7, 11,
  23
  abandons family, 8–9, 19, 138
  death, 126, 141
Hamilton, James Alexander (son),
  97
Hamilton, Philip (son), 92, 95, 140
  death, 128–29
Henry, Patrick, 2, 36
Hessians 88
  Washington's attack on, 55,
    59–63, 67
Howe, William, 49, 53, 56, 70–71,
  77

Independence Hall, 98

Index

Jay, John, 29, 100, 109, 139, 141
Jefferson, Thomas, 2
  vision of America's future, 3, 5,
    114–17
  politics, 119, 121, 124–27,
    136–37

King's College
  fighting unit, 44, 46
  Hamilton at, 28–29, 33, 35,
    41–42, 44, 46, 139
Kortright, Cornelius, 16, 20
Knox, Henry, 56–57
Knox, Hugh
  Hamilton's teacher, 14–15,
    19–20, 22, 26–27

Lafayette, Marquis de, 86–87, 91
Lansing, John, Jr., 98
Laurens, John, 82–83, 88
Lee, Charles, 82–83
Levien, Rachel Fawcett (mother),
  6–7, 10
  business, 8–9, 11
  death, 9, 12, 14, 138
Lexington, Battle of, 2, 41, 44,
  138
Liberty Boys, 44–45
Livingston, Catharine, 29
Livingston, Sarah, 29
Livingston, William, 27–31, 75
Lytton, Peter, 9

Madison, James, 136–37
  vision of future America, 95–96,
    99–101, 104, 106, 108–9, 114,
    116–17, 139, 141
Massachusetts
  battles in, 2, 41–42, 49, 138
Monmouth, Battle of, 82, 140

Nevis island
  birthplace, 6–7, 11, 18, 138
New York, 10, 16, 22, 134
  anti-slavery, 14, 96
  bank of, 96, 139–40
  battles in, 49, 65, 71, 139
  British capture of, 49, 51, 53–54,
    56
  Hamilton in, 2, 25, 28–30, 32–33,
    37, 47, 84–86, 89, 91, 93, 95,
    124, 130, 139
  legislature, 139
  politics, 37, 43, 70, 98–99, 110,
    130–32, 140

Paterson, William, 100
Philadelphia, Pennsylvania, 83
  British occupation of, 71–72,
    77
  Congress in, 38, 70–71, 95
  Constitutional convention in,
    98
Princeton, Battle of, 64–65, 68,
  78, 140
Princeton University, 14, 25, 27,
  35
Putnam, Israel, 56–57

Report on a National Bank, 117
Report on Public Credit, 113
*Report on the Subject of Manu-
  factures*, 119
Reynolds, James, 123
Reynolds, Maria, 123

Saratoga, Battle of, 71, 73, 78, 91
Schuyler, Philip, 43, 46, 53
Seabury, Samuel, 38, 40–41
Sons of Liberty, 33, 36
Stamp Act, 28, 35

St. Croix, 69
  Hamilton in, 8, 10, 13–16,
    18–20, 22–23, 35
  hurricane, 18, 22, 138
Stevens, Edward, 18
Sullivan, John, 94
Supreme Court, United States, 29,
  100, 108

Treasury, United States
  Hamilton as first secretary, 3,
    111–21, 123–24, 136, 139
Trenton, New Jersey
  battle in, 55, 59–65, 67–68

United States
  economy, 5, 97, 111–14, 117,
    119, 123–24, 135
  establishment, 2–3, 5–6, 70
  government, 2–4, 74, 80–81,
    84–85, 93–100, 103–21,
    123–27, 140–41
  national bank, 74, 117–18, 140
  national mint, 117–18, 121

Valley Forge, Pennsylvania, 71–73,
  78, 91

Washington, D.C.
  sites of, 1–2
Washington, George, 5
  army, 2, 42–43, 46, 48–50,
    52–57, 59, 61, 63–64, 67,
    70–86, 88, 90–91, 94, 125,
    136–37139–40
  death, 126, 141
  Hamilton as aide, 43, 65–66,
    68–84, 90, 138, 140
  and new government, 99–101,
    111
  presidential cabinet, 57, 111–12,
    115–16, 119–21, 124
West Point, New York, 80, 91
"Whiskey Tax," 119

Yates, Robert, 98
Yorktown, Battle of, 85–88, 91–92,
  94, 14

page:

4: © Bettmann/CORBIS

15: © Michael S. Yamashita /CORBIS

30: © Bettmann/CORBIS

32: © Scala/Art Resource, NY

48: © Bettmann/CORBIS

50: © CORBIS

59: © Bettmann/CORBIS

75: © CORBIS

87: © CORBIS

101: © The Pierpont Morgan Library /Art Resource, NY

115: © Giraudon/Art Resource, NY

118: © Bettmann/CORBIS

132: © Bettmann/CORBIS

Cover: © National Portrait Gallery, Smithsonian Institution/Art Resource, NY

About the Author

TIM McNEESE is a prolific author of books for elementary, middle school, high school, and college readers. He has published more than 70 books and educational materials over the past 20 years, on everything from Conestoga wagons to the French Revolution. Tim is an Associate Professor of History at York College in York, Nebraska. Previously, he taught middle and high school history, English, and journalism for 16 years. He is a graduate of York College, Harding University, and Southwest Missouri State University. His writing has earned him a citation in the library reference work *Something About the Author*. His wife, Beverly, is an Assistant Professor of English at York College. In 2003 and 2005, Tim and Beverly hosted a college study trip for students that followed 1,500 miles of the Lewis and Clark Trail. They have two children, Noah and Summer. Readers are encouraged to contact Professor McNeese at tdmcneese@york.edu.